Kylie

The Illustrated Biography

Kylie
The Illustrated Biography

MARIE CLAYTON

Trans
Atlantic
Press

Published by Transatlantic Press
First published in 2012

Transatlantic Press
38 Copthorne Road
Croxley Green
Hertfordshire
WD3 4AQ, UK

© Transatlantic Press

All images © Getty Images:

ISBN 978-1-907176-75-3

Printed and bound in China

Contents

Introduction

When Kylie released her first record, the original 1987 version of 'Locomotion' in Australia, it was regarded as just a spin-off to take advantage of her popularity as Charlene in the Aussie television series *Neighbours*. Even when her follow up record, 'I Should Be So Lucky' was released to a much wider audience and was another massive hit, many people confidently expected that Kylie the singer would eventually sink without trace as have so many other promising young chart toppers. Instead her singing career continued to blossom and grow, with hit after hit, and more than twenty years after that first single she is still an international A-list star, with a devoted following of fans in most countries around the world.

What the doubters had failed to take into account was that Kylie not only had the drive and passion to succeed, but also a genuinely good singing voice and considerable stage presence – despite her tiny stature. And however grateful she was to *Neighbours* for giving her a start, she knew she had more to offer than Charlene, which was one reason why she moved on so swiftly from any attempt at typecasting. Even before her well-publicised romance with bad boy rock star Michael Hutchence she was distancing herself from her initial girl-next-door image, and although at first it wasn't cool to like Kylie soon many major players in the music industry were falling over themselves to work with her. Many of her records were also taken up by the gay club scene, and it wasn't long before she was regarded as an undisputed gay icon.

Unfortunately Kylie's public success wasn't matched in her private life; she went through a series of failed relationships and in 2005 was diagnosed with early stage breast cancer. She dropped out of public life for nearly a year during treatment, but when she returned in 2006 with her Showgirl: The Homecoming Tour it was a complete triumph. Since then she has gone from strength to strength and has even found success in America, which previously had been one area of the world where Kylie-fever had never really taken hold. Throughout her career, Kylie has handled both criticism and misfortune with dignity and charm and now pretty much everyone would wish her the ongoing success she deserves. She has certainly achieved credibility as a musician and also something else that might have seemed unlikely at the start of her career: now it's cool to be a Kylie fan.

Part One

I Should Be
So Lucky

A starring role in Neighbours

Opposite and above: Photographs of Kylie, at the start of her career. She was born in Melbourne, Australia, on May 28, 1968, the first daughter of Ron Minogue, an accountant, and his wife Carol. Ron was born and bred Australian, but Carol had come from Wales with her family when she was still a child. Kylie was followed by a brother, Brendan, in 1970, and a sister Danielle, in 1971. Although Kylie was a natural performer, it was her baby sister, known as Dannii, who first became famous. As the main star of the weekly *Young Talent Time*, Dannii rapidly became one of the most recognized children in Australia and Kylie was known for many years as Dannii's big sister. Kylie had small parts in a couple of Australia soaps, but her first big break was a role as one of the lead characters in *The Henderson Kids*. However, it was as the feisty Charlene in *Neighbours* that she finally became a household name, soon eclipsing her sister in the fame stakes. Charlene's on–off relationship with Scott, played by Jason Donovan, caught the imagination of Australian viewers – and when the series was broadcast in Britain it soon caught the attention of those in the UK too.

Singing for charity

Above: The cast of *Neighbours* – with Kylie in the centre – appear at the 1987 Windfield Cup in Sydney. Kylie's singing career came about almost by accident – she and several other *Neighbours* stars had agreed to sing at a benefit in aid of Fitzroy Football Club and Kylie proved to have a great voice. She was soon signed up by Mushroom Records, who put English sound engineer Mike Duffy – on loan from Pete Waterman's studios – in charge of producing what they thought would be a one-off novelty record to capitalize on the massive popularity of *Neighbours*. On July 28, Kylie's first single 'Locomotion' was released; it hit No.1 in the Australian charts within a week and stayed in the top spot for a further seven weeks. It went on to become the best-selling Australian single, not just of 1987 but of the entire 1980s.

Opposite: Kylie with Jason Donovan; Charlene and Scott's fairytale wedding became one of the defining moments of *Neighbours*. The series wasn't the first time the two of them had appeared together – they had played brother and sister in the short-lived Australia soap *Skyways* in 1979, one of Kylie's first roles. They didn't make much of an impression on each other: Kylie said later, 'Both Jason and I looked pretty terrible. He was really chubby with a bowl haircut.', while Jason said of her, 'After filming was wrapped and we said our goodbyes I didn't give her a second thought.'

A singing star

Left: Kylie at the 2nd Annual ARIA Music
Awards in Sydney, with her award for
Highest Selling Single for 'Locomotion'. The
ARIA (Australian Recording Industry
Association) Music Awards celebrate
excellence in the Australian music industry.
After the huge success of her first record,
Pete Waterman of UK 'Hit Factory' Stock,
Aitken and Waterman was asked to provide
a follow up single. Kylie had come to London
on a 10-day promotional tour and on the last
day she arrived at the Stock, Aitken and
Waterman studios to record her new song.
The song was recorded that afternoon, and
by early evening she was on a plane back to
Melbourne. 'I Should Be So Lucky' caused
a sensation when it was first aired on
London's Capital Radio, and the switchboard
was swamped with fans demanding
information about this new singing star.

Opposite: It was also in March 1988 that
Kylie became the first artist to win four
Logies – an Australian television award –
including a Gold Logie for Most Popular
Television Personality on Australian
Television.

Two Gold discs

Left and opposite: At a press conference at Maxim's in London, on July 6, 1988, Kylie was presented with two Gold discs – one for 'I Should Be So Lucky' and the other for the next single, 'Got To Be Certain'. By this time Kylie had decided to move on from *Neighbours* and her last episode was screened in Australia later that month. She had signed up with Terry Blamey Management and had released her first album, *Kylie*, which had debuted in both the Australian and UK charts at No.2.

Everyone wanted to know whether Scott and Charlene's onscreen relationship was a genuine romance in real life. However, although Jason and Kylie had been a couple for several years – and had even been to Bali on holiday together – officially they were just friends. This was partly to retain both stars' public appeal but also because the couple themselves felt that they wanted to keep part of their lives private.

The Loco-Motion re-released

Opposite and right: Kylie in North America in 1988. Kylie's original version of 'Locomotion' had only been released in Australasia, but after the success of
'I Should Be So Lucky' and 'Got To Be Certain', Pete Waterman decided that there was enough interest in the young singer to justify the re-release of her very first record. The song was revamped by Mike Stock and Matt Aitken to sound more like a Hit Factory production, and the title was changed back to 'The Loco-motion', the original title of the song, which was first released by Little Eva in the 1960s. The new Kylie version entered the UK charts at No.2 – a new record for a female artist at the time – and quickly reached No.1 in seven other countries. It was also the first of Kylie's songs to become a hit in the US, where audiences hadn't seen *Neighbours*, debuting at No.80 in the *Billboard* charts but swiftly rising to No.3. It went on to be certified three times Platinum and was her biggest US hit until 2001.

Kylie travelled to London in November 1988 to take part in the Royal Variety Performance. She sang 'I Should Be So Lucky' and then introduced ten of the most prominent members of the cast of *Neighbours*, who had made the trip to London to perform a short sketch that had been specially written for the show. Even though the *Neighbours* episode in which Charlene finally left the series had not yet been broadcast in Britain, Kylie had chosen not to appear in the sketch as she was trying to distance herself from the character of Charlene and move her career forward.

'Most Fanciable Female'

Right: Kylie's third single of 1988, 'Got To Be Certain', did not reach No.1 in the UK, but it did make it into the top 10, while her first album had debuted at No.2 and swiftly reached No.1 – making her the youngest female vocalist at the time to reach the top position in the UK album charts. Her next two singles, the re-release of 'The Loco-Motion' and 'Je Ne Sais Pas Pourquoi', had also reached the No.2 position in the UK singles charts. She had achieved the most incredible success in her debut year as a singer and at the first *Smash Hits* Poll Winners' Party she was awarded Best Female Singer and Most Fanciable Female. Meanwhile Jason Donovan was keen to emulate his girlfriend's success and he also soon signed up with Stock, Aitken and Waterman – although Dannii, Kylie's younger sister, signed with MCA instead.

Opposite: A casual Kylie in London in July 1989.

Keen to be involved

Kylie and her family have always been close and her father's financial training has stood her in good stead. The money she earned was carefully invested from the beginning, and within a year she was a millionairess.

However, before long Kylie was keen to develop her creative relationship with Stock, Aitken and Waterman. She had achieved a string of hit singles with them but as she matured as a singer she wanted to become more involved with the whole creative process rather than be presented with a finished song to learn and sing. Initially she asked if she could collaborate in writing the songs or have some artistic involvement in the accompanying videos, but as Mike Stock, Matt Aitken and Pete Waterman worked as a unit they felt that there was little room for another contributor. Her contract with Pete Waterman's independent record label PWL still had several years to run, so for the time being she accepted their decision.

Especially For You

Left: Jason and Kylie singing their duet, 'Especially For You', which was released in the UK in November 1988. Jason had already released his first solo single with the Hit Factory, which had not done as well as Kylie's efforts, and soon everyone was asking when they would release a single together. Neither was at all keen on the idea, but Pete Waterman convinced both Kylie and Jason that there was such a demand that any song would go straight to No.1.

First million-seller

Right: A duet was written especially for the couple by the Hit Factory, recorded in Sydney at the beginning of November and by the end of the month the record was in the shops. A luscious and truly romantic ballad, 'Especially For You' had already reached Silver status in pre-orders and went on to become the first Kylie record to sell over one million copies.

Feature film debut

Left: On stage early in 1989. Kylie had recently signed up for her first feature film, *The Delinquents*, in which she was to co-star with American actor Charlie Schlatter. It was due to begin filming in Australia in May 1989, the first available break she had in her busy schedule. Based on a best-selling novel by Australian author Deirdre Cash – which was published under the nom de plume Criena Rohan – the storyline was based around the love affair of two teenagers who have to fight their families and then social workers and the police to be together. Although Kylie's character, Lola, was as feisty as the famous Charlene she was much more raunchy and the press were beside themselves at the promise of Kylie naked. The love scenes were reasonably explicit, but much of the film focused on gloomy 1950s Melbourne and the unglamourous world of the Australian correctional system.

Opposite: At Aalsmeer TV studios in the Netherlands in February.

Global success

Left: A publicity still taken at Aalsmeer TV studios in the Netherlands in February. Kylie was popular in many countries in northern Europe right from the start – 'I Should Be So Lucky' had reached No.1 in Belgium, Finland, Germany, Switzerland and Ireland as well as in the UK and Australia, and in many other countries in reached the Top Ten. She also soon had a massive and enthusiastic fan base in the Far East – particularly in Japan and Hong Kong. In fact Kyliemania had taken over Japan – when 'Turn It Into Love' was released exclusively in the Japanese market to meet demand, it instantly shot to No.1 on the Oricon Japanese International chart, and remained there for an amazing 10 weeks – even though there was no accompanying video or much other promotion. At the same time she had four other singles in the Japanese Top 40: 'Especially For You' at No.3, 'It's No Secret' at No.4, 'The Loco-motion' at No.27 and 'I Should Be So Lucky', which by now had dropped to No. 31. Over the 12 month period from December 1988 to December 1989 she had spent an amazing 27 weeks – or almost six months – at No.1 in Japan.

In February 1989 Kylie had also posed for the first time to enable a waxwork model of herself to be made by the famous Madame Tussauds in London. The model was unveiled the following July and soon became so popular that it ended up being the first of several versions of Kylie to appear in the museum. Even though she was still appearing on British television screens as the curly-haired and feisty mechanic Charlene in *Neighbours*, the figure did not portray her in the character of Charlene but in her new persona as a chart-topping and popular singer.

Renewing an acquaintance

Left and opposite: Kylie, and with Ian 'Molly' Meldrum, the Australian music critic, journalist and record producer, at the 1989 ARIA Awards ceremony, which was held in Sydney, Australia. Kylie was there to receive the award for Highest Selling Single again, this time for 'I Should Be So Lucky'. She also became the first artist to receive the newly-created Special Achievement Award. The evening perhaps allowed Kylie to renew her acquaintance with rock star Michael Hutchence – whom she had first met at a party after the Countdown Awards ceremony in July 1987 – since INXS won Best Group and also received the Outstanding Achievement Award.

End of a relationship

Opposite: A publicity photograph from May 1989. Since the relationship between Jason and Kylie had never been official as far as the press was concerned, there were no big newspaper stories when they finally split up, which happened sometime during 1989. They had been growing apart for some time – Jason wasn't ready to settle down, and for Kylie her career had begun to come first. Kylie had already met Michael Hutchence – who would become her next serious love – on a few occasions, although they had not yet begun any kind of relationship.

Right: Performing in Antwerp in November 1990. Kylie's latest single was 'Step Back in Time', which peaked at No.7 in the UK charts. It was taken from her third album, *Rhythm of Love*, which was released that November; it showed Kylie in a more stylish and contemporary light and was the first album to include songs she had co-written. It peaked at No.9 in the UK charts, and at No.10 in the Australian charts.

Disco In Dream

Above: Kylie on *Going Live!* a television show broadcast in the UK during the 1980s. By mid-1989 it had become apparent that Japan couldn't get enough of all things Kylie, so a short tour, the Disco in Dream Tour, was quickly arranged. In comparison with later tours it was an extremely low-key affair – there was no live band, so Kylie performed to pre-recorded music, and the staging was basic. Kylie only performed eight songs, accompanied on stage by a small group of dancers.

The first concert in Japan was at the Rainbow Hall in Nagoya, followed by two dates in Osaka. The final date, and highlight of the tour, was a concert at the Tokyo Dome, which had a capacity of 40,000; it was a resounding success, being feted by the Japanese press as the 'biggest disco in history'. Afterwards Kylie returned to the UK, where the tour continued with a series of ten concerts across the country that also featured other artists promoted by Pete Waterman. The finale was an appearance at the second annual *Smash Hits* Poll Winners' Party, where Kylie performed her latest single, 'Never Too Late', which had just been released. She was also awarded Best Female Solo Singer.

Opposite: Kylie pictured on the 'Formel Eins' television show in Munich.

We met in the middle

Left: When Kylie had met Michael Hutchence for the first time in July 1987, INXS was one of the most famous rock bands in the world while she was still appearing in *Neighbours* and had only released one single, 'Locomotion' – although it was currently No.1 in Australia. They had met again the following year when Kylie and Jason had been invited to a party after an INXS concert in Melbourne. When Kylie travelled to Japan for her first tour in 1989 she stopped over in Hong Kong, and Michael – who had a home there – took her out to dinner. He had recently parted from his girlfriend and Kylie was no longer with Jason, so their relationship soon began to progress. After the final concert in Tokyo Michael turned up at Kylie's hotel unexpectedly, and from that moment on they were a couple. To many it seemed an unlikely partnering: 29-year-old Michael had a reputation for being a womanizer with a rock and roll lifestyle, while 21-year-old Kylie appeared to be the original innocent girl-next-door. However, as Kylie said herself later, 'Michael was not as bad as everyone thought, and I was not as good. We met somewhere in the middle.'

A change of image

Right: Arriving at the Australian
première of *The Delinquents*, Kylie looks
completely different in a cropped blonde
wig; at first everyone thought she was
just an anonymous rock chick, who
Michael had brought to the event for
company. When they realized it was
Kylie, there was an immediate media
frenzy. It was the first time the couple
had appeared in public together, and it
confirmed the rumours of a relationship
were true. The film itself was the box
office No.1 in both Australia and the UK,
although many critics were less than
kind about both the film and Kylie's
performance. In fact she was excellent
in the movie, and revealed an acting
ability and versatility that should have
led to a developing acting career.

Enjoy Yourself

Left: On stage at the London Docklands Arena in April 1990, during the UK leg of the Enjoy Yourself Tour, which was the first real tour – with live musicians – that Kylie had undertaken. It had begun with a concert in Brisbane, Australia, on February 3, followed by two further concerts in Sydney and Melbourne. On home ground she was well received, gaining some good reviews in the press. The play list included Kylie's hits, as well as covers of a few classics such as 'Blame It On The Boogie', 'ABC' and 'Dance To The Music'. After a month off, the tour moved on to the UK where the upcoming single, 'Better The Devil You Know', was added to the encore. This gave the audience – which at the time consisted mainly of very young girls – a taste of the new Kylie that was emerging, a Kylie that was more sophisticated and sexy.

Gaining confidence

Right: The change in Kylie was only partly due to the influence of Michael Hutchence; Kylie herself had already begun to move away from her bouncy and innocent image but Michael gave her the confidence to stand up for herself and take things further and faster. She wanted people to take her seriously as a singer – and she wanted more involvement in what she sang and how she presented it. She had spent time hanging round the recording studio watching INXS create their new album and had learned a lot. As a result, she and her manager, Terry Blamey, went to the US to work with some American producers on tracks for her new album, and she made her own video for 'Better The Devil You Know', which was much more raunchy than anything she had produced with Stock, Aitken and Waterman. The song also had another momentous effect: it was adopted wholeheartedly by the gay audience, and all of a sudden Kylie had become a gay icon.

New influences

Left: Kylie with British singer-songwriter Boy George at the London Fashion Awards in October 1991. The previous year had been perfect for Kylie; her career was moving much more in the direction she wanted, she was a multimillionairess and she was happily in love with Michael Hutchence. Unfortunately her relationship was not to last: after an idyllic Christmas together in Michael's villa in Roquefort Les Pins in the South of France – the first Christmas Kylie had spent away from her family – INXS had gone on tour to promote their new album. There were soon rumours about Michael spending time with other women while he was away – he hated being alone, particularly at night – but there was a more serious threat on the horizon; he had been introduced to Danish supermodel Helena Christensen. By February 1991 Kylie was alone and heartbroken.

Opposite: Kylie and American singer-songwriter Lenny Kravitz pictured in 1991. One legacy of Kylie's relationship with Michael Hutchence was that she had developed a much wider circle of friends.

A gay icon

Left and opposite: Kylie on stage during a concert at the Plymouth Pavilions in October 1991. The records she had released in 1990 and 1991 had continued to move her forward musically; her songs were more mature and the videos sexually provocative in a way that would have been unthinkable even two years earlier. Although this had alienated some fans, it also brought in new ones. The records may not have gone straight up to No.1 any more, but they were still hitting the Top Ten – in fact Kylie was the first artist in UK chart history to have achieved the Top Ten with her first 13 singles. And all three of her singles released after 'Better The Devil You Know' – 'Step Back In Time, 'What Do I Have To Do', and 'Shocked' – had been major hits in the gay clubs. As Kylie said herself later, 'I was more or less adopted by my gay audience... it's wonderful... I think they related to my initial struggle to be accepted as myself. Not to mention my penchant for all things pink and showgirl.'

Her relationship with Stock Aitken and Waterman was not so sunny – as they were not happy with the creative control that Kylie was now exercising not least because her record sales were being affected. However, the Hit Factory itself was less successful than it had been: many of their stars had moved on, the music press was constantly questioning their musical integrity and they were no longer dominating the charts in the same way.

Let's Get To It

Left and opposite: Kylie's first tour of 1991 was the Rythmn of Love, which opened in Australia on February 10, at Canberra Stadium. It went on across Australia, with dates in Perth, Adelaide, Melbourne, Brisbane and Sydney. In March it moved over to Asia, with dates in Singapore, Thailand and Malaysia, finishing with four concerts in Japan. Kylie's new, raunchy image was apparent from the start, with daringly revealing costumes and lots of physical interaction with her dancers. Inevitably this led to comparisons with Madonna, although in reality Kylie was in the process of developing her own style – as any artist who wants to survive must do. When the tour moved on to the UK in October, it was renamed the Let's Get To It Tour since by this time her album of the same name had been released. Again there was criticism in the press who wanted to know where the 'old' Kylie had gone – the truth was she had grown up. As she said herself, '... if I hadn't changed at all they probably wouldn't be interested in me today ... If I was doing exactly what I was doing four years ago I would certainly be bored to tears.'

Final Hit Factory album

Left: Kylie arrives at The Rainforest Ball in June 1992. The event had been organized by Sting and his wife, Trudie Styler, to raise funds for the Rainforest Foundation.

November 1992 saw the release of her final single with PWL, 'Celebration', a cover version of Kool and the Gang's US hit single that had been a favourite of Kylie's when she was a child. That August her first Greatest Hits collection had also been released, which neatly covered her career with the Hit Factory. As well as her more well-known hits, this also included tracks that had only previously been released in Japan or the US, such as 'Turn It Into Love' and 'It's No Secret'. The album made it to No.1 in the UK and No.3 in Australia.

Always professional

Right: It was a good high to go
out on, but now the music press
waited to see who Kylie would
sign with next. Most of the major
record labels were interested, and
it was generally felt that she
would choose one of the big
companies to take her career
forward. And one thing that
people who have worked with
Kylie over the years all agree on is
her utter professionalism. No
matter how tired or overworked
she may be, she always arrives on
time, well prepared and ready and
enthusiastic to work. This was
even true when she was still
filming *Neighbours* but planning
to leave to develop her singing
career.

A hit in the clubs

Opposite: A very happy Kylie, November 1991. She had just released 'Keep On Pumpin' It' – a remix of 'Guess I like It Like That' – which became one of the biggest hits on the club scene in 1991, although it only reached No.49 in the charts.

Above: At the Smash Hits Poll Winners Party in December 1992 in London, Kylie appeared dressed as Elvis Presley. That month she had won the award as Sexiest Person on the Planet, from *DMC and Mix-Mag* magazine.

Part Two

Come Into My World

Signing to a new label

Left: Kylie arriving at Planet Hollywood in London in August 1993. The previous February she had surprised everybody by signing with small independent record label deConstruction, instead of one of the big players. Perhaps the big draw was the chance to work with Brothers In Rhythm – Steve Anderson and Dave Seaman – who were ultra-fashionable and who helped her to create a more mature sound over the next few years.

It was also in 1993 that Kylie met William Baker, who had contacted deConstruction asking if Kylie needed a stylist. At the time he was at college but working part time in Vivienne Westwood's London shop and hoping to move into a career in design. He and Kylie got on well, and soon William became her personal stylist and then creative director.

Since 1991 Kylie had been conducting an on–off relationship with South African model Zane O'Donnell – best known for his physique as featured in a Levi jeans ad and also for his reputation as a ladies man – whom she had met during a shoot for the video of one of her singles. Shortly after a trip to Paris during 1993, they split up for good and Kylie returned home to Australia. In 1993 she was also seen out and about with singers Evan Dando and Lenny Kravitz, as well as actor/model Mark Gerber and London art gallery owner Tim Jefferies – who also had a considerable reputation as a ladies man.

Confide in me

Above: Kylie performing on stage in December 1994 in London. Her single 'Confide In Me' – the first result of her new collaboration with Brothers In Rhythm – had been released that September to almost universal acclaim. It reached No.2 in the UK charts but made No.1 in Australia, where it remained for five weeks, as well as hitting the top spot in New Zealand, Finland, and South Africa. It went on to become Kylie's biggest-selling single of the 1990s. The song had come from her first album with deConstruction, *Kylie Minogue*, which was released two weeks later and featured songs by the Pet Shop Boys and M People, among others. The album made it to No.4 in the UK and No.2 in Australia and was also well received by the critics. The second single taken from it, 'Put Yourself In My Place' was released in November; it only made it to No.11 in the charts but the accompanying video – which featured Kylie recreating the opening scene of the movie *Barbarella* and stripping completely – was a great success with her audience. It went on to win the award for the Best Australian Video at the Australian ARIA Music Awards the following year.

Where The Wild Roses Grow

Above: With Nick Cave in Sydney. Kylie had first met Cave through Michael Hutchence, who was a great friend of his. A fellow Australian, Cave was an intellectual whose work encompassed singing, composing, poetry, prose, photography and film. He had written 'Where The Wild Roses Grow' with Kylie in mind; it tells the story of a man who falls in love with a beautiful girl but then murders her because 'all beauty must die'. Kylie sings the song from the point of view of the dead girl, her higher voice contrasting effectively with his deep baritone. The accompanying video showed Kylie lying lifeless on a riverbank, like Ophelia as painted by Millais, singing to herself as Cave stood over her body and stroked her limbs. It was definitely slightly creepy, but one critic called it 'the perfect love song' and it became a huge hit, as well as winning three ARIA awards.

Opposite: Kylie at the Poetry Olympics at the Royal Albert Hall in London the following year. She had been talked into appearing by Nick Cave but was not listed in the programme; she walked out onto the stage alone, casually dressed, and recited the lyrics to 'I Should Be So Lucky' without any musical accompaniment. It was amazingly successful, with the audience laughing along with Kylie as she embraced her past and acknowledged where she had come from – but also showed just how far she had travelled since.

A serious relationship

Right: With French photographer/video director Stephane Sednaoui in 1996. Kylie had met Sednaoui at a party in July 1995 and a few weeks later they took off for a three-week drive across America in a Pontiac Trans-Am. Kylie was not well known in America, so she felt anonymous and free to be herself; after several weeks in a car together she declared they were in love. Stephane became her next serious relationship after Jason Donovan and Michael Hutchence, since they stayed together for two years. However, due to the pressures of their respective careers and finally split up in 1997, although they remained good friends.

In 1997, Michael Hutchence died suddenly in a hotel room in Sydney. Although their breakup had been painful, Kylie and Michael had since become friends and after his funeral she said, 'I would not have missed our relationship for anything and I miss him.'

Opposite: Kylie during her brunette period. In March 1998 she had finally released her *Impossible Princess* album, after a delay of several months. Unfortunately the first single from the album, 'Some Kind Of Bliss', had been released the same week that Diana, Princess of Wales, had died and although it was promoted extensively it had not sold well. The idea of releasing an album with such a title at that time had also seemed rather insensitive, so Kylie had decided to postpone it until later the following year and release a second single in the meantime in the hope it would do a better job of introducing the album. Unfortunately 'Did It Again' only reached No.14 in the UK charts and No.15 in Australia, although it was certified Gold. The album was released in Australia in January 1998 under its original title, but in the UK it was rather uninspiringly renamed *Kylie Minogue In Europe*.

The move to Parlophone

Right: Kylie at the Six Degrees Bar in London in October 1999, for the launch of *Kylie*, a biography compiled by music journalist Chris Heath. A massive tome full of sumptuous photographs of Kylie – some by professional photographers, others candid snapshots – the book also included thoughts about Kylie from many different people, including Nick Cave, Julie Burchill, Elton John, Baz Luhrmann and Boy George.

By this time Kylie had also signed with a new record label, Parlophone. After the release of just one more album with deConstruction – *Kylie: Greatest Hits*, issued in August 1998 – it was announced that Kylie had decided to leave them. She had not released that much material during her time with them, and what there was had not done that well; what the fans wanted was more material like her old hits and that's what she now planned to give them.

Opposite: On stage with sister Dannii, while performing as part of the Mushroom Records 25th anniversary Telstra Concert of the Century at Melbourne Cricket Ground on November 14, 1998. Kylie had taken some time out from touring in the early 1990s – although making several one-off appearances at festivals – but in June 1998 the Intimate And Live Tour began in Melbourne. Staged in smaller venues – hence the name – the tour had basic staging but was an outstanding success and marked the beginning of the relaunch of Kylie's career.

Off and on the stage

Left: London, August 9, 1999. Kylie Minogue arriving at The Queen's Theatre in London In March 1999 Kylie had appeared on stage herself, but not in the West End. Johnny Kidd, father of model Jodie Kidd, organized an annual cultural festival in the grounds of his estate in Barbados and in 1999 this featured a musical version of Shakespeare's *The Tempest* adapted and produced by Kit Hesketh-Harvey. Kylie had been persuaded to take the part of Miranda, but she refused to sing, wanting to appear in a straight acting role for a change. Although she was surrounded by experienced Shakespearean actors Kylie conducted herself more than adequately, and also found a new boyfriend: Rupert Penry-Jones. They continued to date afterwards, although eventually the pressures of her career again caused the relationship to fall apart.

This year also saw Kylie appearing in two more movies back in Australia: *Sample People,* a low budget feature that achieved poor reviews in Australia and went straight to video in the UK; and *Cut,* a rather gory but amusing horror film, which did much better in Australia and reached No.2 at the box office in France.

Opposite: Kylie with her boyfriend, model James Gooding, in 2001. They met at a party in Los Angeles early in 2000; although James was from Essex in England, he was living in Los Angeles at the time. With James she enjoyed a more 'normal' romance than she had with some of her other boyfriends; cooking Sunday lunch, wandering around antique markets and spending romantic weekends away. Since her split with Stephane Sednaoui she had seen a few other men but none seriously; this partnership looked more promising for the long term. It wasn't long before their relationship was out in the open and speculation about possible engagement and marriage began.

Mardi Gras London

Opposite and right: Kylie on stage at the Mardi Gras in London on July 1, 2000; thousands of people had gathered under alternate sunshine and showers in London's Finsbury Park to celebrate the UK's biggest gay and lesbian festival. Kylie sang her latest release, 'Spinning Around', which had debuted at No.1 in both the UK and Australia – her first single to reach the top spot for many years. The fans were ecstatic that Kylie had come back to doing what she did best: a great pop song. The video for the single featured her wearing a tiny pair of gold lamé hotpants – which not only became legendary in pop history but also focused public attention on the gravity-defying Minogue rear. The *Sun* newspaper in the UK demanded that it be recognized as an official 'national treasure' after their readers had voted it the world's best 'pert posterior'. A million men fantasized about the wearer of those hotpants – and she also gained a new young audience who had not heard her hits in the 1980s and had no preconceptions about what kind of singer she was.

Kylie has always said that she is very proud of her gay fanbase and grateful to them for sticking with her when others did not. She has made many appearances at gay nightclubs, including the G-A-Y at the London Astoria. She also appears at the Sydney Gay and Lesbian Mardi Gras as often as her other commitments allow.

Party in the Park

Right and opposite: On stage at the Party In The Park held at Hyde Park, London, on July 9, 2000. Again the weather wasn't perfect but the fans didn't seem to mind a little rain. Unfortunately, there were problems with the staging throughout the event: the sound system cut out on occasion and the monitors were also temperamental so some artists singing live were unable to hear themselves, which made it difficult to keep in tune or in time with their backing track. Despite this the event was a huge success.

On signing with Parlophone the previous year, Kylie had said that she had taken her time in choosing a new label since she had much that she hoped to achieve. After the experimentation of the previous years she felt that she now wanted to make records that were unmistakably 'Kylie' – and with the release of her new album, *Light Years*, in September 2000, it became apparent that was exactly what she had achieved. Gone was all the experimental material of the last few years; the album was packed with commercial-sounding and instantly catchy songs, many of which went on to become disco classics.

Olympic stars

Nikki Webster, the 13-year-old Sydney Olympics opening ceremony star, with Kylie on top of the Sydney Harbour Bridge in September 2000. The opening ceremony was one of the most spectacular ever, designed to present everything typically Australian, from sea creatures and flora and fauna to Australian cultural icons. It had a cast of 12,687, but Nikki appeared in several of the different segments – most memorably, 'flying' on wires during the Deep Sea Dreaming section. When Kylie first appeared in the closing ceremony, she wore an identical outfit to the one Nikki had worn in the opening ceremony.

Olympic queen

Opposite: At the closing ceremony for the Sydney Olympic Games, Kylie was carried out to the centre of the stadium by hunky lifeguards, sitting on a surf board. As she stepped onto the stage she was surrounded and hidden by her dancers for several minutes, but as her name was announced the dancers parted to reveal that she had changed into a sparkly pink showgirl costume with a dramatic feathered headdress. She first performed Abba's 'Dancing Queen' – which had become associated with Australia ever since it had featured in the iconic Australian film *Muriel's Wedding* – and afterwards her own new single, 'On A Night Like

This'. For much of her performance she was surrounded by 'Kylie' drag queens; there was a thriving club scene in Sydney that often held 'Kylie Nights', with performers dressing up as their heroine. At the end of the ceremony she returned to the stage again to join the other performers in a rousing rendition of that other great Australian anthem, 'Waltzing Matilda'. Although other famous Australian entertainers had appeared at this and at the opening ceremony – including Olivia Newton-John – it was Kylie's performance that was the most memorable.

Above: Performing during the opening of the 2000 Paralympic Games at Sydney Olympic Park on October 18, 2000.

A duet with Robbie

Left: Robbie Williams and Kylie performing their duet 'Kids' on stage at the MTV Europe Music Awards on November 16, 2000 in Stockholm, Sweden; their steamy performance was one of the highlights of the event. Created by Robbie and his writing partner Guy Chambers specifically for Kylie's album *Light Years*, the song also featured on Robbie's album, *Sing When You're Winning* and was released as a single in October 2000.

I loved it

Right: Both stars had said they liked the other in previous interviews, and the chemistry revealed in the video of the song convinced the press that there must be something going on between them in real life, although it was never to happen. That didn't stop Kylie from playing up to the situation: for one early live performance together she appeared on stage wearing a very brief costume that left very little to the imagination. She said of Robbie's reaction afterwards, 'For a second he lost it and I loved it.' The single became her third chart success of the 1990s, reaching No.2 in the UK just as 'On A Night Like This' – the second single from the same album – had done. It was by now very clear to everyone that Kylie's career was firmly back on track.

On A Night Like This Tour

Left: Kylie on stage during a concert in 2001 at the Armadillo in Glasgow, Scotland. Tickets for her biggest world tour to date had gone on sale in December 2000, and had sold out at once. The tour had been scheduled to begin in Dublin, Ireland, on March 1, but instead opened in Scotland on March 3 because serious storms had halted all travel to Ireland. The staging was inspired by legendary Broadway shows such as *42nd Street*, *South Pacific* and the Hollywood musicals. It featured backdrops that included the deck of an ocean liner, an Art Deco New York City skyline, and the interior of a space ship. Many of her old hits were rearranged for the concerts, including 'I Should Be So Lucky', which became a poignant torch song, and a jazzy big band version of 'Better The Devil You Know'. She also introduced 'Can't Get You Out Of My Head', which later became one of her very biggest hits.

Your Disco Needs You

Right: On stage at the Hammersmith Apollo, London, in March 2001. Kylie had recently released 'Your Disco Needs You' – written with Robbie Williams and Guy Chambers – but only in Australia and a few other countries. It was not released in the UK because she was concerned that it was too much like the previous three singles taken from *Light Years* and it had also been a bonus track on the UK release of 'On A Night Like This'. Although the song did not perform as well in the charts as many of her other singles – possibly because by the time it was released the album version had been played excessively – it went on to become a classic performance piece and also a massive hit on the club scene.

Moulin Rouge!

Right: Kylie arriving at the Los Angeles première of *Moulin Rouge!*, which was directed by another famous Australian, Baz Luhrmann. He had wanted Kylie for the cameo role of the green fairy right from the start, and images of her in costume were widely used to promote the film before its release. In the story the hero, Christian (played by Ewan McGregor), meets up with the bohemian set in Paris led by famous artist Toulouse-Lautrec, and together they drink vast quantities of absinthe, a highly alcoholic spirit. This was known to cause hallucinations and was widely believed to be the inspiration – and downfall – of many artists of the period. Its popular nickname was *La Fée Verte* (the green fairy), and after several glasses the assembled company imagine that the green fairy on the side of their bottle has come to life. A tiny Kylie proceeds to flit around the room, singing snatches of several songs and at one point replicating into a row of tiny Busby Berkeley-style fairy dancers. Since her role was largely dependent on the special effects required, Kylie did not work directly with any of the other actors in the film – not even fellow Australian Nicole Kidman, who starred as the doomed Satine.

Opposite: With American musician Huey Morgan of the band Fun Lovin' Criminals on stage at the BRIT Awards at Earls Court, London, on February 26, 2001.

Hit single in the US

Opposite: Kylie at the MTV Europe Music Awards held at the Festhalle, Frankfurt, Germany on November 8, 2001. She opened the show by performing her latest single, 'Can't Get You Out Of My Head', which had been released that September across Europe and in Australia. It debuted at No.1 in Australia, Ireland and the UK and remained there for four weeks in each country, eventually being certified Platinum in the UK and three times Platinum in Australia. In all it hit the top spot in over 40 countries and the following year was released in North America, where it became her second-ever US Top Ten hit when it reached No.7 on the *Billboard* Hot 100.

Until now the one place that Kylie had never had much success was in North America. Her only Top Ten hit there had been 'The Loco-Motion' in 1988; *Neighbours* had not been shown in the US so most Americans had no idea who Kylie was. However, Parlophone had a business arrangement with Capitol records in America, so now all she had needed was the right single — and 'Can't Get You Out Of My Head' was that single.

Right: On stage in at the 'Smash Hits' poll winners party at the London Docklands Arena on December 2001.

Fever

Left: Kylie on stage at the Smash Hits Poll Winners' Party held at the London Docklands Arena in December 2001. The success of 'Can't Get You Out Of My Head' in the United States was followed up by releasing the album *Fever* there in February 2002, some five months after it had been released elsewhere. It was perhaps even more successful in the US than the single, reaching No.3 in the *Billboard* 200 chart and being certified Platinum. It changed the perception of Kylie in the US, where up until now she had been regarded as rather a one-hit wonder. In the UK and Australia it was just as successful, eventually being certified six times Platinum and seven times Platinum respectively.

The relentless schedule of promoting both a hit single and a hit album worldwide had taken its toll on Kylie's health, however. She had always driven herself hard and kept going however tired she was, but it finally came to the point where her doctors ordered her to take a week off, which she had to spend in bed recuperating.

Opposite: With James Gooding at the Palais des festivals in Cannes, France,

A winner at the BRIT Awards

Opposite: Australian actor Russell Crowe presents the award for Best International Female Artist to Kylie Minogue at the BRIT Awards at Earls Court in London in 2002. She also won Best International Album for *Fever*.

Right: Kylie performing live at the BRIT Awards, wearing an eye-catching brief, white Dolce & Gabbana dress. She sang a Doug Crichton remix of 'Can't Get You Out Of My Head' combined with 'Blue Monday', a song that had originally been released by British band New Order in 1983; the revised version of the song was retitled 'Can't Get Blue Monday Out Of My Head'.

James Gooding had escorted Kylie to the awards, but by now their relationship was in trouble. There were rumours that he had a roving eye – he later admitted affairs with model Sophie Dahl and actress Martine McCutcheon while Kylie was away on tour – but also he reportedly found her professional persona difficult to deal with; not only was she the object of countless male fantasies, she was also expert at teasing the press by flirting with her co-stars. It was all a publicity game, which both sides involved understood, but James was said to find it deeply upsetting and felt it somehow negated their relationship. By May 2002 they had split up, although they remained friends and continued to date on and off for almost another year.

KylieFever 2002

Left: Kylie at the 2002 Annual World Music Awards at the Monte Carlo Sporting Club in Monaco. She won the award for Best Selling Australian Artist Of The Year. She also delivered another show stopping performance of 'Can't Get Blue Monday Out Of My Head' to an estimated worldwide audience of one billion people.

The following month saw the start of the KylieFever 2002 Tour, with a concert in Cardiff, Wales, on April 26. The tour covered most of Europe and then moved to Australia, and tickets had sold out within minutes of going on sale. It had a much larger budget than past shows – reportedly costing £4 million to stage – due to the huge success of *Fever* and its related singles, so the stage sets were much more elaborate with two staircases and five projection screens, which were used to enhance the different themes of each segment. The two-hour show featured stunning choreography by ex-Rambert Dance Company Rafael Bonachela, with dancers leaping around in sci-fi inspired costumes looking like robots. In London the tour played four sold-out nights at the Wembley Arena, and in Manchester it broke the record for the most dates played by a solo artist at the Arena, playing to over 85,000 people. In Newcastle, it was announced that Kylie's show had been the quickest to sell out in the history of the venue.

By royal command

Opposite: Kylie looks alluring at The Royal Variety Performance held at London's Hammersmith Apollo in December 2002. The performance raised funds for the Entertainment Artistes Benevolent Fund and was televised by the BBC.

Above: Kylie enjoys the party during the 2002 MTV Spring Break on the beach at the Grand Oasis Hotel in Cancun, Mexico.

On stage in America

Left and opposite: Kylie on stage at MTV's TRL: All Access Week at the MTV Beach House in New Jersey, USA, in July 2002. Total Request Live (TRL) Radio, a countdown of the twenty biggest audience-requested songs of the week, offered unrivalled access to the biggest stars. Kylie appeared during the month-long break between the European and Australian legs of her KylieFever 2000 Tour. There were no plans to bring the full tour over to North America – one reason given was that the staging was designed for large venues, but Kylie was fairly new as a success in the US and it was felt that she was not yet well known enough to generate enough ticket sales to fill the mammoth North American venues. She was also reluctant to scale the show down for smaller venues, so for the moment the US was omitted from the tour schedule completely.

The previous month she had released the third single from *Fever*, 'Love At First Sight', which again did really well. It reached No.2 in the UK and No.3 in Australia and although it peaked at No.23 on the *Billboard* Hot 100, it did make No.1 on the *Billboard* Hot Dance Club Songs. It also reached the Top Ten in many other countries, as well as smashing the airplay record of 'Can't Get You Out Of My Head' with an astonishing 3,116 radio broadcasts in 7 days.

Controversy at Madame Tussauds

Above: On July 3, 2002, a third Kylie waxwork was unveiled at Madame Tussauds in London. This third version showed her kneeling on all fours dressed in the skimpy red dress she had worn at the 14th Annual World Music Awards and long black boots. The model whispered at visitors as they walked by but it was the famous Minogue bottom – almost fully on show in gauzy Agent Provocateur underwear – that attracted the most attention, particularly from young male visitors. Kylie pointed out that although she had indeed worn the dress, and had been photographed in that pose, it was not common sense to put the two together – particularly since onlookers could walk right around behind the model. The following month the back of the dress was lengthened by several inches so that it covered the model's bottom.

Opposite: Kylie arriving at the MTV Music Awards in New York in August 2002. She won the award for best choreography for 'Can't Get You Out Of My Head'.

Outstanding achievement

Opposite and right: Kylie sparkles on stage in Rotterdam during the European leg of the KylieFever tour.

In October that year she won an unprecedented five awards at the 16th Annual ARIA Awards in Australia: the Outstanding Achievement Award, Best Pop Release and Highest Selling Album for *Fever*, and Highest Selling Single and Single of The Year for 'Can't Get You Out Of My Head'. She had also been nominated for Album of the Year and Best Female Artist for *Fever*.

Kylie La La La

Opposite: Kylie appears in the Prince's Trust Performance of *The Play What I Wrote* in London in November 2002. A celebration of the career of British comedy duo Morecambe and Wise, the play featured a different mystery guest each night and on this night it was Kylie. She met Prince Charles backstage after the show and he praised her performance as 'fantastic'. They met again the following month, backstage again, after Kylie had appeared in The Royal Variety Performance at the Apollo Theatre in London, which was held in aid of the Entertainment Artistes Benevolent Fund. It was later reported that Prince Charles had said to her, 'We can't go on meeting like this...'

That same month saw the publication of *Kylie La La La*, a book by Kylie herself and her creative director William Baker. Rather than a traditional autobiography they produced a retrospective of her career, with over 300 beautiful photographs and fascinating text about life with Kylie by William, with additional comments from the woman herself. The fans and most of the press loved the book, although a few journalists complained that she had not revealed anything about her private life. This was deliberate; Kylie was still determined that her personal life would continue to remain as private as possible.

Right: At the KIIS FM Jingle Ball concert at the Honda Center in Anaheim in California, on December 19, 2002. Kylie appeared in the concert along with other stars such as Mariah Carey, Justin Timberlake, and Destiny's Child.

At the Jingle Ball

Left and opposite: Kylie appearing at Z100's Jingle Ball 2002 held at Madison Square Garden in New York on December 12, 2002. The annual concert was arranged by the radio station Z100 – also known as WHTZ – which serves the New York metropolitan area via a transmitter on top of the Empire State Building. Other stars appearing included Ashanti, Beyoncé and rapper Ja Rule. Kylie was appearing in several Jingle Ball concerts that December instead of taking her KylieFever 2002 Tour to North America.

She had several other live engagements scheduled while she was in America, including an appearance to perform 'Come Into My World' on *Good Morning America*. It was not a massive success; her erotic dance sequence was perhaps a little racy for the rather conservative audience of a morning news and current affairs show.

Kylie during Z100's Jingle Ball
2002 - Show at Madison Square
Garden in New York City, New York.

Tonight with Jay Leno

Opposite: Kylie performing on *The Tonight Show with Jay Leno* at the NBC Studios in Burbank, California, on December 20, 2002.

Above: Film star Cameron Diaz, presenter Jay Leno and Kylie on *The Tonight Show with Jay Leno*. It was Kylie's third appearance on the show that year; she had been featured on February 4, along with Arnold Schwarznegger – at that point still a leading film star, since he had not yet begun his campaign to become Governor of California – and also on

July 12. After the success of *Fever* and its related singles in the US Kylie was now making a concerted effort to conquer North America and appearing with established US stars was part of the strategy. That same month she also appeared at MTV's Total Request Live (TRL) at MTV Times Square Studios in New York City, along with American actor Denzel Washington.

A more casual Kylie

Opposite: Actor Joel Edgerton and Kylie watch the Women's Doubles final at the Australian Open Tennis Championships at Melbourne Park in Australia in January 2003. Joel had appeared in *Sample People* with Kylie a few years previously, but was most famous for his role as the young Luke Skywalker's uncle in *Star Wars Episode II: Attack Of The Clones*.

Left: Kylie performs on the *Tonight with Jay Leno* show in 2002.

Causing a sensation at the BRITS

Opposite and right: American pop star Justin Timberlake gets a handful of the most famous rear end in the world during a duet on stage at the BRIT Awards at Earls Court in London in February 2003. Despite the impromptu look of the move, it had been carefully rehearsed to maximize media coverage of the two stars performing a raunchy dance routine to a medley of Justin Timberlake's hit 'Cry Me A River' and Blondie's 'Rapture'. Afterwards Justin said, 'She's got the hottest ass I've ever seen. On a scale of one to ten it was a fifty-eight.' And as for Kylie, she gleefully told reporters, 'We had to rehearse that. I was like, "Wait, I don't think we got that quite right. I think we should do it again!"' It all had its desired effect; neither singer had won anything at the event, but they certainly won the publicity stakes next morning, with more column inches devoted to them than to any of the award winners.

After the performance Kylie and her sister Dannii had dinner with Justin and then he went back to his hotel, the Mandarin Oriental, where Kylie reportedly joined him for a night of passion. In reality she was only there for a few hours and was probably just avoiding her by now very-ex boyfriend James Gooding, who had made a jealous public scene after the awards event and had then gone to wait for her for half the night outside her Chelsea home. He later checked himself into rehab, but then sold a sensational story of his three-year relationship with Kylie to the UK newspaper *The News Of The World*.

At the GRAMMYS

Opposite: Kylie Minogue and Justin Timberlake at the 45th Annual GRAMMY Awards on February 23, 2003. In the UK Kylie was better known than Justin and their duet had provided him with valuable publicity. In the US the position was reversed and Kylie took advantage of Justin's popularity to boost her own image in North America.

Left: Kylie arriving at Madison Square Garden in New York for the 2003 GRAMMY Awards.

February 2003 also saw the UK launch of Kylie's range of underwear, LoveKylie, at Selfridges in London. Although professional models wore the designs for the press launch, Kylie herself was featured modelling them in a video that was played in one of the store's windows on Oxford Street. The items in the range were designed by Kylie herself, who wanted to offer women the opportunity to spoil themselves saying, 'there's nothing wrong with a little indulgence!'. The styles came in a variety of colours, with beautiful fabric and lavish trim detail and the range quickly became a brand with a devoted following.

Enter Olivier Martinez

Opposite: Kylie with French actor Olivier Martinez in Monte Carlo in May 2003. Olivier was not only regarded as the answer to US heart throb Brad Pitt in France, but was also becoming known in Hollywood after having played a lead role in the movie *Unfaithful* with Richard Gere and Diane Lane. He had moved to the United States at the end of the 1990s and he and Kylie had met in New York in February after the GRAMMY Awards. They were quickly photographed out and about together – for once Kylie appeared quite open about her personal life and did not try to keep the relationship secret.

Left: Kylie and Bono of Irish band U2 meet up at the 48th Ivor Novello Awards in London in 2003.

Kylie was currently working on new material for her next album at Biffco's studios in Dublin. The first single from this, 'Slow', was not to be released until November, but it quickly jumped to the top of the charts in both the UK and Australia. It also gave Kylie her third No.1 in the *Billboard* Hot Dance Club Songs chart, although it only just managed to scrape into the *Billboard* Hot 100 chart. It was very well received by the music critics, but surprisingly it did not sell that many copies – in fact it was one of the lowest-selling No.1 singles in UK chart history.

A developing romance

Left: Kylie with boyfriend Olivier Martinez in London. During 2003 the couple travelled to the Côte d'Azur, where Kylie had spent time with Michael Hutchence in the past. Within a short time Olivier and Kylie had become a recognized couple, and there was soon talk about marriage and children in the press. However, Kylie still seemed wary of trusting her man – not surprisingly perhaps, since several of her previous serious relationships had ended because of her partner's infidelity. It didn't help that Olivier was soon on location making a film with beautiful American film star Angelina Jolie – before she met Brad Pitt – and the two of them had quickly become friends. Kylie flew out to visit the set, perhaps worried that the rumours of a budding relationship were true; if so she was presumably reassured since she and Olivier remained an item.

Body Language

Right: A photocall to promote the album *Body Language*, Cologne, October 2003. The album was due out on November 17 internationally and on February 10 in North America. The cover featured Kylie looking very French and rather like a young Brigitte Bardot – a new image that had been unveiled at the first performance of 'Slow' on BBC television's *Top Of The Pops*. The songs on the new album were all very different from those on *Fever*; Kylie had moved on to a more 1980s electro funk sound. It had mixed reviews from the critics – some loved it, others dismissed it as a 'mis-step' after her previous album. At least one reviewer thought that the problem was that the only stand-alone track was 'Slow' – the rest of the album worked best when taken as a whole, although listening to it in that way was a truly luxurious and seductive experience. *Body Language* didn't do quite so well as *Fever* – it only reached No.2 in the Australian albums chart and No. 6 in the UK, but was still certified two times Platinum in Australia and Platinum in the UK.

MTV Music Awards

Left: Performing 'Slow' at the MTV Europe Music Awards on November 6, 2003.

Opposite: Kylie arriving at the MTV Europe Music Awards, which were held in a specially-erected tent at the Ocean Terminal, Edinburgh, with the spectacular Edinburgh Castle as a backdrop. Kylie was one of the nominees for Best Female, but this year she lost out to Christina Aguilera, while Best Pop – the other award for which she was nominated – went to Justin Timberlake.

The *Body Language Live* DVD included a short documentary that followed Kylie behind the scenes as she prepared for the Money Can't Buy concert in London and the launch of the album. One thing it shows clearly is how hard Kylie works, fitting in rehearsals for the show alongside all her other commitments.

Money Can't Buy

Opposite: Kylie performing in a one-off show at the Hammersmith Apollo in London on November 15, 2003, to promote her album *Body Language*. The million-pound special was a free concert – tickets could not be bought but were given away in competitions on the radio, TV and Internet. However, many of them fell into the hands of ticket touts, who sold them on at vastly inflated prices. Kylie's stunning and graphic black and white costume had been designed by Jean-Paul Gaultier – it heralded the French theme of the entire show.

The songs were a mixture of tracks from the forthcoming album and a selection of her established hits, such as 'On A Night Like This', 'Can't Get You Out Of My Head', and 'Spinning Around'.

Above: Fashion editor Glenda Bailey, Kristin Scott Thomas, Kylie Minogue and stylist William Baker at the Chanel Haute Couture Spring/Summer 2004 show in Paris. Kylie had always been very interested in fashion – when she was a young girl she had wanted to have her own clothing line. That month a 12-inch high, fully poseable Kylie doll had been launched at the London Toy Fair. The doll was available in two different outfits – the red mini dress as featured on the infamous wax model at Madame Tussauds and the silver two-piece from KylieFever 2002. Both outfits also had matching LoveKylie knickers.

A constant support

Above: EMI Music Vice Chairman David Munns, Kylie Minogue, EMI Music Chairman Alain Levy and Kylie's manager Terry Blamey at the GRAMMY awards in February 2004. Terry had been Kylie's manager right from the start and although he was rarely featured in the press he was always there for her, controlling her image and stepping in to order relaxation time when it was obvious that she was driving herself too hard.

The following month the second single from *Body Language* was due to be released: 'Red Blooded Woman'. It debuted at No.5 in the UK and went up to No.4 in Australia, and this time in the US it made it right to No.24 in the *Billboard* Hot 100 and to the top spot on the US Dance Airplay Chart.

Opposite: Performing at the 46th Annual GRAMMY Awards show in Los Angeles. It was a big event for Kylie since she had won her very first prestigious GRAMMY award: Best Dance Recording for 'Come Into My World' from the album *Fever*.

Fans' favourite

Left: Kylie performs at the BBC *Top of the Pops* Concert in December 2004.

Opposite: Singing her latest single, 'I Believe In You,' during the Smash Hits Poll Winners' Party at London's Wembley Arena in November 2004. Readers of the teen magazine voted for their favourite stars and Kylie received the lifetime achievement award for her 17-year contribution to the music business.

Showgirl – The Greatest Hits Tour

Opposite: Arriving at the 6th Annual White Tie & Tiara Ball, an annual charity event to benefit the Elton John Aids Foundation sponsored by Chopard and held at Elton John's Old Windsor home. June 2004 also saw the release of 'Chocolate' – the third and final single from *Body Language* – a rich, slow and seductive ballad that unaccountably failed to sell as many copies as it deserved. Meanwhile, Kylie had already moved on again and was currently working on new material for her next album, *Ultimate Kylie*, which would be a collection of her greatest hits from across her entire career.

Above: Kylie at the microphone during a surprise visit to DJ presenter Johnny Vaughan on the Capital FM Breakfast Show, in Leicester Square, London, on October 19, 2004. She was there to launch her new single 'I Believe In You', which was due to hit the stores in December. It was one of only two new tracks from the album *Ultimate Kylie,* which had been released in September and was an outstanding success, reaching the Top Ten in the album charts across the world. Kylie had also recently announced that her Showgirl – The Greatest Hits Tour would begin in March 2005. The fans were so eager to see her live that several websites selling the tickets were so overloaded they crashed and all the venues were quickly sold out.

Branching out

Opposite: Kylie performing on *Wetten, Dass..?* (Want to Bet?), a German television show, on December 11, 2004. In November she had also made two guest appearances on the cult Australian TV series *Kath & Kim*, which was an outrageous comedy about the superficial lives of divorcée Kath Day and her spoilt daughter Kim. One of Kylie's episodes featured a flash forward, and she plays Kim's dim and sulky daughter, Eponney Rae, preparing for her wedding day in a hilarious send up of Charlene's wedding in *Neighbours*. Kylie was obviously having a ball in the over-the-top part, and also revealed an unexpected gift for comedy.

In December 2004 she had another rather unexpected part: Madame Tussauds created a celebrity Nativity scene, with David and Victoria Beckham as Joseph and Mary, George W. Bush, Prince Philip and Tony Blair as the Three Wise Men, and Samuel L. Jackson, Hugh Grant and Graham Norton as shepherds. Above them all floated Kylie as a very beguiling angel.

Right: At *The Magic Roundabout* UK charity premiere, London in January 2005. Kylie was the voice of Florence in the movie.

Meanwhile, Kylie was preparing for the start of her tour. She had always pushed herself hard and had suffered exhaustion in the past, but this time she seemed to feel really tired all the time. However, when she began getting cold sweats as well, and being sick on a regular basis, it was decided it was time she saw a doctor. She submitted to a whole barrage of tests, then went back to work while she waited for the results.

Triumphant tour

Right: On stage at Earls Court in London on May 1, 2005, and (opposite) in Paris during the Showgirl – The Greatest Hits tour. The tour had opened in March with five concerts in Glasgow, then travelled to major cities in northern Europe before returning to the UK and finishing the European leg with seven nights in London. The biggest and most spectacular Kylie tour to date, it featured £5 million pounds worth of lighting effects and a vast, five-part hydraulic stage with revolving sections.

Doctors break bad news

Opposite and right: During the tour Kylie herself had seven costume changes and wore outfits by leading designers, including a blue, jewel-encrusted corset by John Galliano that made the most of her curvy figure. It was widely reported to have given her a 16-inch waist, but Kylie herself said, 'A 16-inch waist? Wow! Even I would be amazed!' The shows featured versions of all her big hits and the tour was a massive success – in the opinion of the *Times*, it was 'the gig of the year'.

After the final European show, Kylie and Olivier Martinez flew to Australia to spend time with her family before the Australian leg of the tour began. It was here that doctors broke the news that she had early stage breast cancer. Within a few days the remainder of the tour had been cancelled, and Kylie had been admitted to St Francis Xavier Cabrini hospital in Melbourne to begin treatment.

Part Three

Better The Devil You Know

June 2006: In remission

Above: Kylie with flowers given to her by *News of the World* reporter Rav Singh in London in May, 2006. After the cancer was diagnosed, Kylie had had a partial mastectomy in Australia to remove a tumour in her left breast and had then opted to go to the Institut Gustave-Roussy in Paris for the follow-up chemotherapy. She wanted to 'have a life with my boyfriend in Paris' but in reality she was often so desperately ill that she couldn't get out of bed. Many had expected that Olivier would not stick around through the trauma, but he was one person who could relate to what Kylie was dealing with, since he had nearly died himself in a motorbike accident when he was younger. He cancelled his other commitments so he could be there to support her and when she began to feel better again he took the first pictures to be posted on her website. Early in 2006 she was well enough to return to Australia to begin back-up radiation therapy. By June it was announced she was in remission – although it would be several more years before she was officially free of cancer. One of the goals she had set herself when she was really ill was to be well enough to return to her favourite restaurant in Portofino, which she and Olivier managed to achieve that July.

Opposite: Kylie Minogue arrives at the *Brasil Brasileiro* premiere at Sadler's Wells Theatre in London in August 2006.

Back in the limelight

Opposite: Kylie had lost her long hair early in her treatment, but according to reports she had taken this in her stride – perhaps because she had changed her look often during her career anyway. With her cropped blonde hair, she looked very like the rock-chick who had been photographed with Michael Hutchence at the premiere of *The Delinquents*, way back in 1989. She said later that she was thrilled when her eyebrows and eyelashes began to appear again – she had been afraid that she would be one of the few patients who never managed to grow them back. What she found more upsetting than the hair loss was the way she kept forgetting things when she was undergoing chemotherapy – she had to start keeping a diary of her medication.

Right: When she appeared on stage to introduce the Scissor Sisters, who were performing a free gig at Trafalgar Square in London on September 16, 2006, everyone could see that she now seemed to be glowing with health. She was already rehearsing to resume her postponed Showgirl tour now her energy was coming back. Although some people thought she should be taking it easy, she wanted to return to normal life as quickly as possible – and for her, normal life was to be out there performing.

The Showgirl Princess

Opposite: At a signing of Kylie's book for children, *The Showgirl Princess*, at Waterstone's Oxford Street in London in September 2006. Many of the 250 young fans who were lucky enough to meet her had won their tickets in various competitions. Kylie said that she had always loved to write, but that in the past her other commitments had taken up too much of her time. The book had been very satisfying to work on during her treatment when she was too weak to perform. The story of the showgirl princess was based on elements from her own life, including the appearance of Sheba, her boyfriend Olivier's dog, who she said had been comforting to cuddle when she was feeling down in Paris during her illness. The illustrations used photographs of Kylie as the main character, cleverly combined into the main artworks by illustrator Swan Park.

Right: At a photo call on November 8, 2006 in Sydney, Australia, to launch her new fragrance, Darling by Kylie, which had been produced in association with Coty. It was her first official appearance in Australia since her treatment had finished.

On the road again

Left: Kylie arrived in Australia from London in November, 2006. to begin Showgirl – The Homecoming Tour, which was due to kick off on November 11 in Sydney. Since the original Showgirl tour had covered the UK and northern Europe but had been cancelled before it could open in Australia, this time she would tour Australia first. There were 20 concerts scheduled across five cites before Christmas, then after Christmas the tour moved to the UK for another 13 concerts, 7 in London and 6 in Manchester. The new tour was not the same as the original: as well as introducing new designs, some of the dance sequences were revised and longer breaks were introduced between the different segments, since Kylie was not physically capable of sustaining the frenetic pace of the original. Many of the costumes were also redesigned since she could no longer wear the originals.

Showgirl – The Homecoming

Opposite and right: Kylie on stage for the opening night of her Showgirl – The Homecoming Tour at the Sydney Entertainment Centre on November 11, 2006. She told the audience, 'I'm used to being fashionably late, usually by ten minutes. Today I'm a year and a half late.' The show was a triumph, with critics describing it as the perfect comeback. Much of the material had been heard before but there was one new song, 'White Diamond', taken from material being recorded for a new album that would not be released until a year later. Most of the shows on the tour were just as successful, but on what would have been the second night in Manchester the show had to be cancelled 45 minutes in. Kylie had been suffering from flu, which had developed into a respiratory tract infection, and she had to be carried from the stage. Typically she was concerned at having let the fans down, while almost of them were worried about whether the cancer had returned. She was taken to hospital and the following two scheduled shows were postponed, but within a week she was back – and an additional show was added to the end of the run, specifically for the fans who had missed out when she left the stage early.

Kylie – The Exhibition

Left: Kylie and her Creative Director and stylist William Baker arriving at the opening night of Kylie – The Exhibition at the Victoria & Albert Museum in London on February 6, 2007. Kylie had donated over 600 costumes and other memorabilia of her career to the performing arts collection based at the Arts Centre in her home town of Melbourne. She said that the only reason so many of them had survived was because her mother, Carol, had stored them away since the start of her career in the 1980s. Carol had been a talented dancer when she was young but had never wanted to pursue it professionally, preferring marriage and family life instead. When Kylie began touring, Carol had begun working backstage helping the dancers and she had saved Kylie's costumes at the end of each tour. The Melbourne Arts Centre decided to mount an exhibition to showcase fifty of the most memorable outfits from across Kylie's career, which had first gone on show in Melbourne in the first four months of 2005. The exhibition had then moved on to do four-month stints in Canberra and Brisbane, finishing with a six-month run in Sydney. After closing down for the final six months of 2006, the exhibition had been remounted for a tour of the UK, beginning with London and then moving on to Manchester and Glasgow. It finally closed towards the end of January 2008.

Just three days earlier it had been announced that Kylie and her boyfriend, Olivier Martinez, had split up after four years together. When she began appearing in public again after her illness, she had said of him: 'He was always there, helping with the practical stuff and being protective. He was incredible. He didn't hesitate in cancelling work and putting projects on hold so he could be with me. He's the most honourable man I have ever met.'

A career in clothes...

Above: The exhibition in London opened to the public on February 8. It contained more material than the original, and was divided into seven sections that covered clothes and stage outfits, shoes, awards, record sleeves, Silver/Gold/Platinum discs, videos and a reproduction of Kylie's dressing room from the just completed Homecoming tour. Items on display included the overalls Kylie wore as Charlene in *Neighbours*, the famous gold lamé hotpants featured in the 'Spinning Around' video, the white hooded jumpsuit from her video of 'Can't Get You Out of My Head' and some of the fabulous corsets featured in the original Showgirl tour. Kylie commented, 'Each and every item in this collection evokes a myriad of memories and marks a time and place in my life.' She was also reported to be very amused to see garments that had once been thrown on the floor during quick costume changes backstage suddenly being handled with reverence by specialists in white gloves.

New ventures

Right: Kylie arriving at the Shanghai venue for her concert to promote the launch of Swedish fashion retailer H&M's first store on mainland China in April 2007.

Opposite: On stage during the opening of H&M's flagship store in Shanghai. The H&M range for summer 2007 was inspired by Australia and had a relaxed, sporty, beach-life feel, mixed with lots of shiny metallic for a more glamorous look. It included a limited line of bohemian-chic beachwear, H&M loves Kylie, and the star herself was the face of the beachwear advertising campaign. Ten per cent of all money spent on the Kylie beachwear line was donated to WaterAid, an international charity dedicated to the provision of safe domestic water, sanitation and hygiene education to the world's poorest people.

in May 2007. Kylie had recently confirmed rumours she would be starring in the popular UK science fiction TV series *Doctor Who* – a part was being specially written for her in the forthcoming Christmas Special. The idea had been suggested by her stylist William Baker, who had been a great fan of the series for many years. Kylie played a waitress called Astrid on the *Titanic*; not the doomed liner, but a cruise spaceship orbiting above Earth, ready to teleport wealthy passengers from around the galaxy down to London to experience a traditional English Christmas. The episode was filmed in July in great secrecy and the chemistry between the two leading characters was very obvious.

Working on new material

Above: Kylie and her sister Dannii with Mark Webber of Australia and Red Bull Racing, posing for photographers during a visit to the Formula One paddock area before the Australian Grand Prix at Albert Park in Melbourne in 2007. Dannii had been engaged to racing driver Jacques Villeneuve in 1999, but after 18 months the couple had split up. However, as Kylie had said of past relationships, 'I don't regard them as failures. You aren't going to find Mr Right by sitting at home. You have got to go out and try a few.'

Kylie had not released any records since 2005, but she was hard at work on new material. In March several songs appeared on the Internet, supposedly taken from recording sessions with Kylie. In May another three songs appeared, and some journalists accused Kylie of deliberately leaking material to build up hype for her new album, which was due to be released later in the year. Kylie denied the charge and said that, as far as she could recall, she had never recorded any of the songs in question.

Opposite: Arriving at the Dolce & Gabbana party at the Cannes Film Festival in May 2007.

Q Idol Award

Above: Kylie and her manager Terry Blamey raise a glass at the Q Awards party at the Grosvenor Hotel in London on October 8, 2007. The Q Awards are annual UK music awards that have been run every year since 1990 by the music magazine Q. The awards ceremony has become one of the biggest and most highly publicized in the UK, perhaps partly due to the boisterous, and sometimes outrageous, behaviour of some of the celebrities who attend.

Opposite: Kylie with Q Idol Award, for successfully returning to the music industry after beating breast cancer, which was presented by Alan Carr and Justin Lee Collins. Her win was greeted with a standing ovation from the celebrity audience and in her speech she said, 'Just don't ask me what it means, but I'm very grateful and honoured to be receiving this.' She went on to thank her manager and everyone for continuing to support her.

White Diamond

Opposite: Kylie arriving for the UK premiere of *White Diamond* in Leicester Square, London, on October 16, 2007. The documentary commemorated the preparations for Showgirl – The Homecoming Tour, including behind the scenes footage at some of the concerts, and had been made between August 2006 and March 2007. It had been directed by William Baker, perhaps the only person who could have convinced her to do the project. The portrait that emerged of Kylie was of a charming woman who was loved by pretty much everybody – there were no scenes of her swearing, losing her temper or behaving like a diva in any way. The scenes of her on stage were shot in colour, while others were in black and white – a device that Madonna had also used in her infamous backstage documentary, *In Bed With Madonna*. The title song, 'White Diamond', had originally been written by the Scissor Sisters for Kylie's forthcoming album but had since been dropped from the final track listing – although it was the only new song that had been added to the revised Showgirl tour. Critical response to the documentary was mixed – some critics seemed almost disappointed that it did not reveal any backstage bad behaviour.

Right: Kylie and her sister Dannii at the premiere. Kylie was also accompanied by William Baker and actor Rupert Everett.

Music Industry Awards

Opposite: Kylie arriving at the Music Industry Trust Awards at the Grosvenor House Hotel in London on October 29, 2007. She was to receive the Music Industry Trust's Award in recognition of her 20-year-career, and was both the first woman in the event's 16-year history to receive the award and the youngest artist to date to receive it. David Munns, Chairman of the Award committee, said: 'There is no doubt that of our 15 Award recipients to date, Kylie is by far the most glamorous. She deserves this award for her success over 20 years, staying at the top in one of the toughest professions and inspiring millions with her grace, dignity and humanity.' The ceremony was held in front of 1,200 guests and raised money for the Brit School and Nordoff-Robbins Music Therapy.

Left: Kylie performing her new single '2 Hearts' for the first time, with Jake Shears of the Scissor Sisters, during the Music Industry Trust Awards. A report of the event in the UK newspaper *The Telegraph* pointed out that Kylie also currently held the record for the most-played female artist on UK radio.

The Kylie Show

Opposite: Kylie leaving the George V Hotel in Paris on November 10, 2007. That evening the UK's ITV channel broadcast *The Kylie Show*, a combination of her singing and a series of hilarious skits based on the apparent view of the tabloids that the 'real' Kylie must be very different to her 'smiley Kylie' public persona. She is obviously having a ball as she pretends to be an alcoholic, foul-mouthed diva, addicted to gambling and watching reruns of her wedding scene in *Neighbours*. In one memorable skit she and Dannii have an over-the-top catfight backstage and when Simon Cowell appears and assumes that Kylie is Dannii's mother, she lets fly at him with her famous Charlene right hook. The ending provided a truly unexpected punchline – collapsed in her dressing room at the end of the show, Kylie peels off a rubber face to reveal she is really that flamboyant villainess, actress Joan Collins. Two days later Kylie released her latest single '2 Hearts', which she had described as 'glam-rock meets *Cabaret*'. It debuted in the UK at No.12, but quickly leapt up to No.4, thus becoming her 14th consecutive Top Ten hit in the last seven years. In Australia it went straight to the top spot, becoming her 10th No.1 there.

Right: A photo call to launch the new album *X* – because it was her 10th – at the Hotel de Rome in Berlin, Germany, on November 22, 2007. It had gone straight to No.1 in Australia and No.5 in the UK, but Kylie said later that she wasn't 100 per cent happy with it: 'In retrospect, we could definitely have bettered it, I'll say that straight up. Given the time we had, it is what it is. 'Wow', 'In My Arms', 'The One' and '2 Hearts' are crackers. They go off like a frog in a sock.'

A triumphant end to 2007

Above: American actress Renee Zellweger and Kylie on the German TV show 'Wetten, dass..?' (Want to Bet?) in Graz, Austria on December 8, 2007. In the show ordinary people offer to perform a bizarre or difficult task and celebrities bet on the outcome, usually having to perform a mildly humiliating or funny activity if they lose. However, Kylie was on the show to perform her song '2 Hearts'; rising star Mika also appeared to sing his first single, 'Relax, Take It Easy'.

Opposite: Kylie performing during the prestigious Nobel Peace Prize Concert at Oslo Spektrum in Norway on December 11, 2007. Looking rather Goth in a skintight black dress, black fingerless gloves and black ankle boots, she opened the show with '2 Hearts' and then sang 'Can't Get You Out Of My Head'.

On December 29, 2007, the Queen's New Year's Honours List was announced and it was revealed that Kylie had won a prestigious award of her own – an OBE (Order of the British Empire) for services to music.

Wow

Opposite: Kylie unveils a curly new hairstyle during the Goldene Kamera Awards in Berlin, Germany, on February 6, 2008.

Above: A dazzling performance at the BRITs at Earls Court, London, in February 2008. Kylie sang her new single, 'Wow', dressed in sparkly gold and surrounded by a troupe of dancers dressed from head to toe in shimmering red or blue tracksuits, topped with matching helmets that obscured their faces completely. The second single released from the album X ,'Wow' had rather mixed reviews but it was a success commercially, going to No.5 in the UK charts and No.1 on the UK club and airplay charts, eventually becoming her best selling UK single since 2002. It was only released in the US to American dance radio stations, but it made it up to No.19 in the *Billboard* Hot Dance Club Songs chart.

Kylie had not yet found a steady boyfriend after splitting with Olivier Martinez. When asked if she was looking for love again she said, 'There's always a call to my office saying, "Who's she with?" and my manager's like, "Are you sure you're not with anyone?" and I'm like, "No, but if you can get me someone that'd be great!"'

2008 BRIT Awards

Kylie signs autographs for her fans as she arrives at Earls Court exhibition centre in London for the BRIT Awards. The show was hosted by the Osbournes; Ozzy was delighted to introduce Sir Paul McCartney, the undoubted star of the show and a man he said had inspired him to get into music in the first place.

During the show Kylie presented the Outstanding Contribution to Music award to Sir Paul. She had appeared with him before, on December 31, 2007, on *Jools Holland's Annual Hootenanny*. The two of them had sung his single 'Dance Tonight' as a duet and afterwards Sir Paul had said, 'She's awfully good'.

A delighted David Tennant presented Kylie with the International Female Solo Artist Award, her third BRIT award.

Dressed to thrill

Opposite: Opening night at the Odyssey Arena, Belfast, June 26, 2008 during the KylieX2008 tour. Kylie sports an outfit inspired by a bell boy uniform.

Right: Towards the end of the show, Kylie performs in a costume inspired the clothing of 19th century coachmen at the O2 Arena in London.

KylieX2008 Tour

Above: Kylie performing on stage at the Odyssey Arena in Belfast, Northern Ireland on June 26, 2008. The concert was the first in the UK leg of the KylieX2008 Tour, which had opened in Paris on May 6. The multi-million pound tour was one of her most expensive to stage to date and was described as 'one of the great performances of the early 21st century'. Each show was divided into seven acts plus an encore and interlude. However, it continued to evolve throughout the course of the tour, with changes to the running order, the costumes, set list and even Kylie's hairstyle. The main stage was minimalist, with an illuminated video floor and a backdrop of gigantic moving video curtains. Kylie said that parts of the show had been inspired by those of Queen: 'I'm

releasing my inner Freddie Mercury...' Tickets for the original eight shows of the UK leg had sold-out in just thirty minutes, and eventually more than twenty-five shows were scheduled in England, Northern Ireland and Scotland. Some media pundits wondered if Kylie was up to such a punishing schedule, but she pointed out that the tour was organized so that she did two nights in a row and then had one night off to protect her health.

Opposite: Kylie on stage during the Berlin concert at the Velodrom on June 22, 2008. When she first appeared on stage in the eye-catching spiderwoman dress, she was perched inside a ring like a giant spider in a web. The dress was changed later in the tour.

Kylie OBE and French Chevalier

Opposite: On July 3, 2008, Kylie attended a ceremony at Buckingham Palace to receive her Order of the British Empire (OBE) from the Prince of Wales for services to music. For most recipients of such an honour this means a polite handshake, a curtsey and conversation lasting a few seconds – but Prince Charles spoke to Kylie for an unprecedented 33 seconds, which was something of a record in investiture terms. And Kylie demonstrated a little Australian informality when she said goodbye, clutching Prince Charles's outstretched hand in both of hers – a technical breach of etiquette that left him smiling. Kylie had worn an eye-catching

Yves Saint Laurent dress and five-inch gold heels to Buckingham Palace, and was accompanied by her mother Carol and father Ron.

Above: Kylie poses with her mother Carol and her father Ron after French Minister For Culture Christine Albanel made her a Chevalier dans l'ordre des Arts et des Lettres (a French cultural distinction in recognition of a significant contribution to the arts and literature) in Paris in May 2008. Kylie said, 'I am deeply honoured to be recognized in this way. French culture has influenced me greatly and I have always had colossal respect for the arts and people of France.'

Start of a new relationship

Opposite: At the Fendi 'O' party at Le Milliardaire club in Paris to celebrate burlesque star Dita Von Teese's birthday in October 2008, Kylie meets Spanish model Andrés Velencoso. One of the top male models in the world, Andrés had been the face of leading brands such as Chanel, Louis Vuitton, and Banana Republic and the two of them hit it off immediately. It was not long before he was firmly established as the new man in Kylie's life.

Above: Kylie performs live for the first time in the Middle East at the landmark Grand Opening of Atlantis, The Palm Resort and the Palm Jumeirah in Dubai, United Arab Emirates in November 2008. Earlier that month she had appeared in a concert in Colombia – her first in Latin-America – despite the country's reputation as a dangerous place to visit. While in Bogota, she had received presidential-style security with 15 around-the-clock armed guards, and had travelled everywhere in bulletproof cars with motorcycle escorts.

Home comforts

Above: Kylie on stage during the second section of the KylieX2008 Tour, doing the splits while being carried aloft by four of her dancers dressed in American football costumes. In this section she sang 'Heart Beat Rock', 'Wow' and 'Shocked'.

Stars are often famous for their outrageous demands for things that must be provided backstage – known as riders – but when asked by a journalist on the Australian *Sunday Herald* what hers were, Kylie was hard pressed to think of anything. 'I'm quite boring really,' she admitted. 'As long as I have the kettle, the tea, the coffee maker...' When pressed,

she finally offered, 'I had my own road cases made, which I love. They symbolize home on the road. Every venue I turn up to, there they are and I know my things are in them; personal things you might have in your cupboards at home. I fill them to bulging point. They're made by the same people who make the cases for all the lighting and sound equipment, so they're very roadie, but mine are pale pink.'

Opposite: Performing at the Vector Arena in Auckland, New Zealand in December 2008. According to her official website, the tour grossed an estimated US$70 million in ticket sales in 2008.

Sexy darling...

Left: With host Richard Wilkins during the official launch of her new fragrance Sexy Darling at the Myer City Store in Sydney in December 2008. Richard invited child singer Alana Quartly to sing with Kylie onstage during the event.

December also saw the release of the album *Kylie Boombox*, which contained remixes of many of Kylie's previous big hits but had no new material.

Opposite: Kylie waves to fans as she arrives at the launch. Fans in their hundreds had packed the store to catch a glimpse of her. The Australian section of her KylieX2008 Tour was due to begin three days later with the first of three concerts at the Acer Arena in Sydney. She was then due to perform three concerts in her home town of Melbourne, before taking a break over Christmas with her family. Her sister Dannii had recently told a UK magazine that their Christmas was a real family affair and that their routine hadn't changed since they were kids. She said, 'It's so exciting. Christmas is all about the kids. Kylie and I love to spoil our nephews, but we still have stockings. It's a two-day event for Christmas Day and Boxing Day – there'll be at least four cousins and their partners, uncles, aunts and then the grandparents. It's like a festival – it should be called Minogue Fest.'

Kylie didn't forget those who were going through the same ordeal as she had three years previously; before her final show in Melbourne she took some time to meet with 10 young cancer patients backstage.

A new romance?

Opposite: Kylie with British comedian James Corden on stage during the BRIT Awards at Earls Court in London in February 2009. Comedian Mathew Horne was also a presenter and the three of them performed a quick spoof version of 'Can't Get You Out Of My Head', the men dressed in red satin drag outfits and Kylie in a diaphanous white Alexander McQueen Grecian gown. Kylie had filmed a cameo for the pair's comedy sketch show, *Horne And Corden*, the previous year and there had been rumours that she and Mathew were dating. However, he eloquently denied that they were ever an item in the UK newspaper *The Sun*: 'The idea of people camping outside my mum's house last year to ask her if I'm seeing Kylie is ridiculous. Of course nothing happened ... she's Kylie.' He went on to say that of course he fancied her...

Right: Kylie, showing her continuing interest in fashion, is pictured at the Jean-Paul Gaultier collection show in Paris. The sexy 2001 ad for Agent Provocateur lingerie in which she had stripped to her underwear and ridden a mechanized rodeo bull had recently been voted the best cinema ad of all time. The racy advert had topped an online poll by Digital Cinema Media.

Bollywood debut

Above: Kylie poses arm in arm with Indian Bollywood actor Akshay Kumar, flanked by Lara Dutta and Zayed Khan on the right and Sanjay Dutt on the far left, during a press conference in Mumbai for their upcoming film *Blue* in March, 2009. For *Blue*, an underwater extravaganza that was partly shot in the Caribbean, Kylie had been paid a reported US$1 million to play herself – she had a scene with Akshay and sang two songs with Sanjay, Lara and Zayed – and was the first international A-list star to sing for a mainstream Bollywood music director. At a press conference she explained that although she had been singing and acting all her professional life, this time it was different. 'The technical aspects are much the same. It's just that this is not part of an album. And being in the studio with Rahman is magical, he's on the crest of a wave, but is such a generous spirit, very welcoming, he's relaxed and calm... such a nice person,' she said.

Opposite: The previous month the Australian newspaper the *Sydney Daily Telegraph* had reported that Kylie's relationship with her new love Andrés Velencoso had begun to get serious – apparently he had taken her to Spain to meet his family. His mother had died some years previously, but his father owned a bar and restaurant in the Costa Brava resort town of Tossa de Mar.

On top of the world

Opposite: Kylie atop the Empire State building in New York City on May 7, 2009, after switching on the lights to turn the building red and white in a special ceremony in honour of the Coty/DKMS Linked Against Leukemia Partnership, a charitable drive which promotes bone marrow donations. The event was followed by a fundraising gala to raise money for the campaign. It had also recently been announced that Kylie would be the face for Spanish jewellery firm Tous, and she was beginning preparations for her first ever North American tour which was due to kick off in Oakland, California at the end of September.

Above: Performing during the season closure party of the winter resort at Ischgl, Austria, in May 2009. The party was held at lunchtime on Saturday May 2, the closing weekend of the Tyrolean resort. The annual season closure concert is held in a natural bowl near the top station of the main Silvrettabahn gondola from the centre of the village, and is free for those with lift-passes – which are necessary to reach the venue. About 20,000 people attended the 2009 concert, and Kylie performed material from her KylieX2008 Tour.

Perfect for men...

Opposite: Kylie on stage at the opening concert of the Mawazine International Music Festival in Rabat, Morocco, in May 2009. Again she performed her KylieX2008 Tour material for the concert. The Mawazine Festival also hosted an array of other artists from around the globe, including Stevie Wonder, bossa nova master Sergio Mendez and the Algerian diva Warda Al Jazayria.

Above: Arriving for a special performance in aid of the Miracle Africa International Foundation Charity, sponsored by Chopard, during the Cannes Film Festival. Kylie had also just launched her first fragrance for men, Inverse, which was described as being 'the perfect fragrance for a complex man. A fresh, ambery oriental, this beautifully constructed fragrance offers surprising masculine notes that are strong yet sensitive.' The adverts starred her boyfriend, Andrés Velencoso.

Glamour Woman of the Year

Left: Kylie arriving at the Dolce & Gabbana Party at Cannes.

Right: With Formula One driver Jenson Button, who had presented her with the Woman of the Year award during the Glamour Women of the Year Awards 2009 in London. She had also won the Entrepreneur of the Year award.

The following month Kylie was interviewed on *The Today Show* in America to promote her forthcoming US tour. Presenter Kathy Lee Gifford asked why she had never toured in the US before and Kylie replied that she had wanted to many times, but that her management always seemed to have some reason why it wasn't the best time. In the end she had just decided to go for it, so they had set up this special tour even though it wasn't promoting a specific album.

A powerful brand

Left and opposite: Kylie Minogue on stage for MTV Day 2009 at Plaza de Toros de Las Ventas in Madrid, Spain, in July 2009. She looked as stunning as ever in a Jean-Paul Gautier black dress, fishnet tights and knee high boots, with scarlet red lipstick and nail varnish – as well as an unusual glittering silver face mask.

Kylie night

Above: Kylie and Dannii Minogue pose with Jason Donovan and members of the cast of *Priscilla, Queen of the Desert* at the Palace Theatre in London in June 2009. The two sisters had come to support Kylie's ex-boyfriend and longtime friend, who played the leading role of drag queen Anthony 'Tick' Belrose in the show. The production paid homage to Kylie in its script, and even included her 1994 hit 'Confide In Me.' The original 1994 film, *The Adventures of Priscilla, Queen of The Desert* – an Australian cult classic – was to have had a Kylie song as the finale but at the time it was decided that Kylie was not famous enough in the US to sell the film, so it became an Abba song instead. Some thought that the original premise had been inspired by the famous 'Kylie Nights' in Sydney – when drag queens dress up and perform as Kylie. Kylie herself said later that the first she heard about 'Kylie Night' was when one of her friends mentioned it during a trip back to Australia early in her career, but that she hadn't actually seen herself being impersonated until she was taken to see a show in a club in her home town of Melbourne in 1993.

Opposite: The launch of a new bed linen range for Kylie at Home.

Thank you for the music

Kylie with Benny Andersson of Abba performing during Thank You For The Music – A Celebration Of The Music Of Abba at Hyde Park in London in 2009. The cast of the London stage version of *Mamma Mia* also took part in the show. Kylie was the star attraction at the concert, performing their 1980 hit 'Super Trouper' as well as singing 'When All Is Said and Done' with Benny Andersson – she had described the chance to perform with him as 'a dream come true'.

That November Kylie came in at No. 20 in a list of the 25 Most Influential Australians, which had been published to celebrate *Good Weekend*'s 25th Anniversary Issue. When questioned about why Kylie was selected, Geoffrey Blainey, one of the eight judges, pointed out that Kylie made the list not only for 'showing what the girl next door could do', but for being a powerful role model for women's health.

September 2009: A first tour of North America

Opposite: Kylie on the opening night of the For You, For Me Tour, her first tour to cover North America. The initial concert was held at the Fox Theatre in Oakland, California on September 30, 2009. For 'Like A Drug' she descended to the stage perched on top of a giant diamante-covered skull. Fans had queued around the block to get into the venue – with at least one local newspaper dubbing it 'Kylie-fornia'. The show attracted a good response from American critics, but Kylie and her manager, Terry Blamey, were thrilled with the reaction of fans. He said after the show: 'I've been at every show and this is maybe the best to date. It was certainly the biggest audience response we've ever seen. What a welcome to America!'

Above: On stage during the tour, at the Pearl Theatre in the Palms Resort & Casino in Las Vegas, Nevada in October 2009, wearing an outfit by Jean-Paul Gaultier. Since fans in North America had not seen any of the previous tours, this one was made up of the best bits of each. Despite concerns that it was not financially viable to do the tour, it grossed more than US$3 million over just nine concerts – and although Kylie had said in interviews beforehand that she didn't have that many fans in the US, overall the venues were 97 per cent sold out. After being 'stunned by the glitz and glamour of Kylie's tour and the power it had to pull in celebs when she performed at the Palms', Vegas promoters had even offered her a complete residence for a show in the city.

Anyone for golf?

Opposite: Kylie and Andrés Velencoso leaving her Chelsea home in London for lunch together in January 2010. It had recently been reported in the news that Kylie had bought a luxury villa near the Spanish town where Andrés' family lived.

Above: In London in January 2010. Kylie had also recently taken up golf so she could play with Andrés and had quickly become addicted to the game. In an interview with Australian women's magazine *InStyle* she

had said, 'Golf can be sexy. For me it's been great to do with Andrés in the fresh air for hours. And golf courses are normally attached to very beautiful hotels with beautiful spas and a Michelin star restaurant. You play golf, you relax, you eat. You would be surprised by the people who play golf.' She even joked about putting together her own range of golf clothing: 'Maybe I need to get into designing golf wear because let me tell you it's not easy to look good on the golf course.'

Arriving at the Brits

Right: Cat Deeley and Kylie arriving at the BRIT Awards 2010, at Earls Court in London in February 2010. Some four years earlier, in July 2006, Cat had interviewed Kylie for an exclusive broadcast on Sky One, which was later syndicated around the world. In the interview Kylie had spoken frankly about her treatment for breast cancer and how there were days when she couldn't face looking at herself in the mirror. She also said the experience had completely changed her outlook on life: 'You're stripped down to near zero, but it seems that most people come out the other end feeling more like themselves than ever before.'

Kylie had recently joined Rod Stewart, Robbie Williams, Leona Lewis and Mariah Carey – among many others – to record the charity single 'Everybody Hurts' in aid of victims of the Haiti earthquake. The record had been organized by producer and music executive Simon Cowell.

Opposite: Kylie performs at the Wind Music Awards Show at the Verona Arena in 2010.

A new mother

Above: Kylie posing with sister Dannii, who had received the TV Star of The Year award at the *ELLE* Style Awards 2010. Dannii had recently announced that she was expecting her first child, and Kylie was thrilled to become an aunt again – their younger brother, Brendan, a cameraman back in Australia, already had two children. Kylie herself had always said she wanted children, and before the chemotherapy and radiation required to deal with her breast cancer she had undergone special treatment that was designed to give her a chance of becoming a mother at some point in the future.

Opposite: Kylie at a charity event in London. In March it was announced that she was to be the new face of a breast cancer charity campaign. She had posed draped in just a silk sheet for pictures taken by acclaimed photographer Mario Testino, which were to be used to launch the new Fashion Targets Breast Cancer (FTBC) campaign for Breakthrough Breast Cancer. Actress Sienna Miller and supermodel Claudia Schiffer had also posed for the campaign.

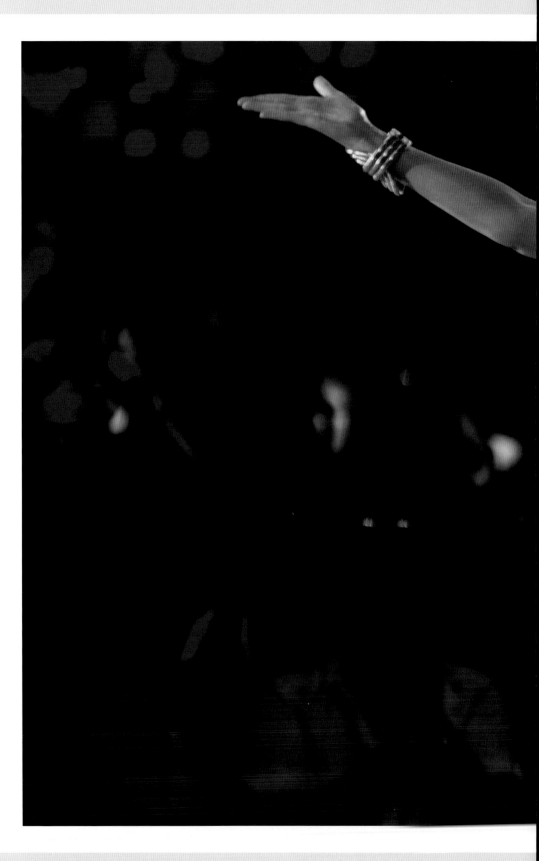

All the Lovers

Opposite: Kylie performs her new single 'All The Lovers' during the final of the TV show *Germany's Next Top Model* at the Lanxess Arena in Cologne, Germany, on June 10, 2010.

She had used Twitter to give fans a sneak preview of the new song, sparking a fan frenzy that crashed her website. Her tweet had directed followers to the official site to listen to a short clip of 'All The Lovers' in April, but the rush of interest was much bigger than she had expected. Minutes later she tweeted again to say, 'Aaahhhhhhhh... you've overloaded the system!!! That is the strength of your combined power!!!!!!! OMG!!!' The single was finally released as a digital download on June 13, and then as a hard copy in July at around the same time as her latest studio album, *Aphrodite*. When asked about 'All The Lovers' in an interview, Kylie had said, 'The single was one of the last tracks to be written for the album. As I was recording it, I knew that 'All The Lovers' had to be the first single; it sums up the euphoria of the album perfectly. It gives me goose-bumps, so I'm really excited to hear what everyone thinks of it.' It turned out to be a great success, praised by the critics as a classic Minogue single. It also did well commercially, hitting the Top Ten in more than 14 countries, as well as reaching No.1 in the *Billboard* Hot Dance Club Songs chart.

Appearing at Glastonbury

Opposite and above: Kylie performing with Jake Shears and Ana Matronic of the Scissor Sisters on the Pyramid Stage at the Glastonbury Festival in Somerset, England, in 2010. Now Europe's largest music festival, Glastonbury showcases some of the world's best artists from all areas of music and performance and was celebrating its 40th anniversary. Kylie had been scheduled to perform in 2005 but she had to pull out due to her illness. This year she appeared in a cameo performance as a special guest with American group Scissor Sisters, receiving a huge ovation when she stepped onto the stage to join them in a revealing black lacy body suit and diaphanous cape. The three of them sang 'Any Which Way', a track from the new Scissor Sisters album, *Night Work*. Scissor Sisters frontman Jake Shears had been working with Kylie on her new album, *Aphrodite*, which was to be released the following month. Touted as a 'celebration of her dance floor roots', Kylie's album had been produced by acclaimed British electronic artist and songwriter Steve Price.

Hey Hey, It's Saturday

Opposite: Kylie arrives at Australia's Channel 9 Studios in Melbourne in July 2010. Her appearance to sing on the TV show *Hey Hey, It's Saturday* was her first performance on Australian television in 10 years. On the show Kylie performed her newly-released single, 'All The Lovers', accompanied on stage by 25 dancers; her London-based choreographer had flown in to Melbourne to oversee the number, which was based on the song's sexy video. The muscular men stripped down on stage to black briefs – or 'budgie-smugglers', as one reporter called them – while the girls ripped off their shirts to reveal cutaway leotards beneath; it was all rather steamy. Afterwards Kylie sang a second track from her new album *Aphrodite*, 'Get Outta My Way'. The album had debuted in the Top Ten in 13 different countries and had became Kylie's fifth No.1 album in the UK, making her the first solo artist in the history of UK charts to have a No.1 album in four different decades.

Above: Kylie performs on stage at G-A-Y Heaven on July 11, 2010 in London.

Last Song of Summer

Opposite and above: Kylie and Rufus Wainwright performing onstage at The Last Song Of Summer Concert at The Watermill Center in Water Mill, New York in August i 2010. The two were singing together for the first time; the concert also included DJ Rachel Chandler to spin in between sets. Kylie wore a stunning strapless leopard-print Dolce & Gabbana fish-tail gown, teamed with an elaborate necklace and jet-black nails, while singer-songwriter Rufus looked like a true rock star in shiny leather trousers and an open white shirt. The two sang a number of duets, including 'Can't Get You Out of My Head', 'The Loco-motion', and 'Somewhere Over the Rainbow'. Their performance was to benefit The Watermill Center, founded by Robert Wilson, which supports emerging artists and creatives.

Globetrotting diva

Left: Kylie at the Emilio Pucci womenswear fashion show during Milan Fashion Week in 2010.

Opposite: With Roberto Cavalli at the Roberto Cavalli 40th Anniversary party at Les Beaux-Arts de Paris in France, on September 29, 2010.

In October Kylie was in Egypt performing a unique concert in a spectacular setting in front of the Sphinx and the Giza pyramids. The event was in celebration of the 10th anniversary of *Enigma* Magazine with profits going to the We Owe It Io Egypt Foundation for the Abou Rish children's hospital. The following day she was off to Mexico to promote her album *Aphrodita*, while November saw her in North America.

Aphrodite hits the US

Opposite: Kylie poses in Mexico City during the promotion of her new album *Aphrodite* in October 2010. The following month she and Dannii were treated to a 'flash mob' dancing tribute in Australia; dancers and supporters of the two sisters had descended on Sydney Opera House to surprise tourists. Dressed as their heroines, the crowd danced to a medley of their hits, including Kylie's 'Step Back in Time' and Dannii's 'I Begin to Wonder'. Both sisters had been delighted when they saw footage of the event on YouTube.com.

Above: In November Kylie appeared in the 84th Annual Macy's Thanksgiving Day Parade in New York City in America. Warmly wrapped up in a Chanel coat and a stylish turban hat, she performed her latest single 'Get Outta My Way' and waved to the cheering crowds. She had told fans beforehand that she would be wearing the most clothes she had ever donned in public for the parade, to make sure that she was family friendly. A few complained later that she was miming the words – but she swiftly pointed out that all the featured artists had to mime.

Aphrodite tour

Left: In 2011 Kylie embarked on the Aphrodite World Tour, which travelled to Europe and Australia as the Aphrodite Les Follies tour and Aphrodite Live in North America, Asia and Africa. A DVD of the concert, filmed in London, was released at the end of November. Here she performs with dancers at the Sydney Entertainment Centre in June 2011.

Jubilee celebrations

Above: French actor Denis Lavant poses with Kylie during the photocall to publicize *Holy Motors*, which was presented in competition at the 65th Cannes film festival. An exhilarating, mysterious odyssey through the streets of an eerie, beautiful Paris that delves deep into the murky relationship between film and our dreams, *Holy Motors* was directed by Leos Carax and starred Lavant, Édith Scob and Kylie – the soundtrack also featured her performing an original song 'Who Were We?' written by Carax and Neil Hannon.

Opposite: Kylie performs on stage during the Queen's Diamond Jubilee Concert outside Buckingham Palace in London on June 4, 2012. The star-studded musical extravaganza took place on the third of four days of celebrations to celebrate Queen Elizabeth II's 60 years on the throne. Kylie was in the midst of her own year-long jubilee celebrations to celebrate her 25 years in the music industry; during the course of her career to date she had released seven No.1 singles and sold over 10.1 million singles in the United Kingdom, making her the 12th best selling singles artist in UK history.

Chronology & Discography

CHRONOLOGY

1968

May 28: Kylie Ann Minogue is born in Melbourne, Australia.

1979

Kylie lands her first acting role, a one-off appearance in short-lived Australia soap *Skyways*.

1980

Eight episodes of Australian war-time drama *The Sullivans* feature Kylie as a Dutch orphan.

1985

Kylie appears as a troubled child in one episode of Australian soap *The Zoo Family*.

May: A new series, *The Henderson Kids*, begins on Australian television. Kylie has a leading role.

After *Neighbours* moves from 7 Network to Network Ten and is revamped, Kylie wins the part of a new character, Charlene.

1986

Feb 24: Kylie begins filming *Neighbours* at Melbourne's Nunawading Studios,.

Apr 17: The episode of *Neighbours* featuring Kylie's first appearance as Charlene is broadcast in Australia. She is an instant hit with audiences – and her on-screen romance

with Scott (Jason Donovan) is soon also being played out in real life.

Aug: The stars of *Neighbours* appear at a benefit for Fitzroy Football Club in Melbourne. Kylie sings lead vocals, and performs so well that she is soon offered the chance to make a record.

Oct 27: *Neighbours* is first screened in the UK.

1987

Apr: Kylie becomes the youngest artist ever to win Most Popular Actress in Australia at the Logie Awards, a prestigious annual Australian television award.

May: Kylie is signed by Mushroom Records, Australia's leading record company.

Jul 1: The *Neighbours* episode featuring the wedding of Scott (Jason Donovan) and Charlene (Kylie) is first broadcast in Australia. This episode was eventually screened in over 50 countries.

Jul: Kylie signs up with Terry Blamey Management, who has continued to manage her career to date.

Jul 19: At a party after the annual Countdown Awards, Kylie meets Michael Hutchence, lead singer of INXS, for the first time.

Jul 28: Release of Kylie's first single 'Locomotion', which went on to become the best-selling Australian single of 1987.

Dec 29: A follow-up single, 'I Should Be So Lucky', is released. It is the first of many Kylie records produced by the Hit Factory of Stock, Aitken and Waterman.

1988

Mar: Kylie becomes the first artist to win four Logies, including a Gold Logie for Most Popular Television Personality on Australian Television.

Mar 29: At the 2nd Annual ARIA Awards, Kylie wins Highest Selling Single for 'Locomotion'.

Jul 1: Kylie performs a one-off show at the Canton nightclub in Hong Kong, the venue is completely sold out.

Jul 4: The first album, *Kylie*, is released. Debuting at No.2, within a month it has reached the No.1 spot.

Jul 6: Kylie receives two Gold discs – one for 'I Should Be So Lucky' and the other for her third single, 'Got To Be Certain'.

Jul 26: The *Neighbours* episode featuring Kylie's last appearance as Charlene is broadcast in Australia. This episode was screened in the UK on Nov 1, 1989.

Nov 28: Following public demand Kylie releases a duet with Jason Donovan 'Especially For You', which for many years is her biggest selling record. However, her relationship with Donovan is now drawing to an end.

1989

Feb: Kylie poses for a wax model of herself at the world famous Madame Tussauds in London.

Mar 6: At the 3rd Annual ARIA Awards, Kylie wins Highest Selling Single for 'I Should Be So Lucky', as well as the Special Achievement Award.

Apr: Filming begins on Kylie's first movie, *The Delinquents*.

Sep: While in Hong Kong Kylie has dinner with Michael Hutchence. It marks the start of an ongoing relationship.

Oct 2: Start of the short Disco in Dream Tour of Japan, which covered Nagoya, Osaka and Tokyo. It finished on Oct 9.

Oct 15: The Disco in Dream Tour moves to the UK, with ten concerts across the country that also featured other artists promoted by Pete Waterman.

Dec: Kylie joins a host of other stars for the Band Aid 2 recording of 'Do They Know It's Christmas' to raise money for Ethiopia.

Dec 21: At the Australian première of *The Delinquents*, Kylie is accompanied by Michael Hutchence and unveils a new rock-chick image with micro-mini and cropped blonde hair.

1990

Feb 3: Start of Kylie's Enjoy Yourself Tour, with a concert in Brisbane. It covers Sydney and Melbourne, and then in April moves on to Britain and Europe, finishing with two concerts in the Far East.

Mar 26: At the 4th Annual ARIA Awards, Kylie wins the Outstanding Achievement Award.

Apr: The video for the new single, 'Better The Devil You Know', features a raunchy Kylie writhing suggestively.

May 26: Last concert in the Enjoy Yourself Tour, in Bangkok.

Dec: Michael Hutchence and Kylie spend Christmas together at his farmhouse in Roquefort-les-Pins in the South of France.

1991

Feb: Kylie and Michael Hutchence break up after he becomes involved with young supermodel Helena Christensen.

Feb 10: The Rhythm Of Love Tour kicks off with a concert in Canberra. The tour covers Perth, Adelaide, Melbourne, Brisbane and Sydney in Australia and in March has dates in Singapore, Thailand and Malaysia finishing with four concerts in Japan.

Mar 10: Last concert in the Rhythm Of Love Tour, at Fukuoka, Japan.

Oct 25: First concert in the Let's Get To It Tour, at Plymouth in England. The tour was a revamped version of the Rhythm Of Love Tour and covered six more dates in England and two in Scotland, finishing with a concert in Ireland.

Nov 8: Final concert in the Let's Get To It Tour, at Dublin in Ireland.

1992

Mar 25: Kylie is nominated as Best Female Artist at the ARIA Awards in Sydney, Australia but loses out to Deborah Conway.

Apr: Top Of The Pops features Kylie performing her new single, 'Finer Feelings'.

May 31: Kylie performs at The Rhythm of Life Fashion Ball in aid of the Rainforest Foundation at the Grosvenor House Hotel in London. The event was hosted by rainforest campaigners Sting and Trudie Styler.

Aug 22: The compilation *Kylie: Greatest Hits* is Kylie's final collaboration with the Hit Factory of Stock, Aitken and Waterman, since she

had now fulfilled her 5-year contract. Kylie had decided to move on; she wanted to be more involved with the creative process and to take her career in new directions.

1993

Feb: Kylie signs with new record label deConstruction, a British independent specializing in dance and pop soul.

William Baker, a young theology student working part time at the Vivienne Westwood store in Chelsea, meets Kylie and goes on to become her stylist.

1994

Feb: Kylie performs at the Sydney Gay Mardi Gras, before an audience of over 19,000.

Jun: Filming begins in Thailand for *Streetfighter*, in which Kylie plays Lieutenant Cammy.

Nov 21: The video for 'Put Yourself In My Place' features Kylie recreating the opening scene of the movie *Barbarella* and stripping completely. The following year the video won the award for the Best Australian Video at the Australian ARIA Music Awards, although the highest chart position the single reached was No.11.

1995

Jul: Kylie meets French photographer Stephane Sednaoui and begins a relationship with him.

Oct: A duet with Nick Cave & The Bad Seeds 'Where The Wild Roses Grow' becomes Kylie's 23rd consecutive top 20 single in the UK. It is later voted Best Song of the Year and wins over a more alternative audience.

Oct 20: At the 9th Annual ARIA Awards, Kylie wins Best Video for 'Put Yourself In My Place' and is nominated for Best Female Artist.

1996

Jan 12: The movie *Biodome* is released, in which Kylie plays Dr Petra von Kant. It does not do well at the box office and in Australia goes straight to video, despite Kylie's presence.

Jul: Kylie appears at the Poetry Olympics at the Royal Albert Hall in London. She is unbilled, and appears on stage unexpectedly to recite the lyrics from 'I Should Be So Lucky'.

Sep 30: At the 10th Annual ARIA Awards, Kylie and Nick Cave win Single Of The Year, Song Of The Year and Best Pop Release for 'Where The Wild Roses Grow'.

1997

Mar: Kylie appears as herself in a *Men Behaving Badly* sketch for Comic Relief.

Nov: The relationship between Stephane Sednaoui and Kylie comes to an end.

1998

Jun 2: Start of the Intimate And Live Tour, with a concert in Melbourne. It covers the major cities in Australia, and finishes with three concerts in England.

Jul 31: Last concert on the Intimate And Live Tour, held in London.

Oct 7: Kylie unveils an updated waxwork model of herself at Madame Tussauds in London.

Nov 14: Kylie and her sister Dannii perform on stage as part of the Mushroom Records 25th anniversary Telstra Concert of the Century at Melbourne Cricket Ground in Australia.

1999

May: Kylie signs with Parlophone in the first step on her musical comeback and soon begins work on new material.

Oct 21: UK launch of *Kylie*, a photographic record of her career to date.

Dec: In East Timor Kylie entertains the Australian troops who form part of the peacekeeping force.

2000

Jan: At a party in Los Angeles Kylie meets British model James Gooding, who later becomes her next serious boyfriend.

Mar 2: The horror move *Cut* is released, in which Kylie has a small part as Hilary Jacobs.

May 11: The Australian movie *Sample People* is released, in which Kylie stars as Jess.

Jun 19: Release of 'Spinning Around', the first single from Kylie's new studio album *Light Years*, which debuts in both the UK and Australian charts at No.1.

Jul 1: Kylie appears at the Mardi Gras, London.

Jul 9: Kylie performs at the Party In The Park, in Hyde Park, London.

Sep 11: The follow up single 'On A Night Like This' repeats the success of 'Spinning Around'.

Oct 1: Kylie performs for millions at the closing ceremony for the Olympic Games in Sydney, Australia.

Oct 9: The third single from Light Years, Kylie's duet with Robbie Williams, 'Kids' is released and is also a chart success.

Oct 18: Kylie performs for millions at the opening ceremony for the Paralympic Games.

Oct 24: At the 14th Annual ARIA Awards, Kylie wins Best Pop Release for 'Spinning Around' and is also nominated for Best Female Artist.

Nov 16: Robbie Williams and Kylie appear to sing their duet at the MTV Europe Music Awards in Stockholm, Sweden.

Dec: Tickets go on sale for Kylie's first major

tour in nine years, On A Night Like This, and sell out immediately.

2001

Feb: Kylie appears in a Pepsi commercial in Australia.

Mar 3: Start of On A Night Like This Tour, with a concert at The Armadillo in Glasgow, Scotland. The tour had been scheduled to start in Dublin, but storms prevented travel so the concert there was cancelled. The tour covered venues in England, Wales, Denmark, Germany and France and then moved on to Australia.

May 15: Last concert on the On A Night Like This Tour, held in Sydney, Australia.

Sep 3: UK première of *Moulin Rouge!* in which Kylie has a cameo role as The Green Fairy.

Oct: Kylie's new album *Fever* debuts in the UK and Australia at No.1, later being awarded triple platinum in both countries.

Oct 30: At the 15th Annual ARIA Awards, Kylie wins Best Pop Release and Best Female Artist for Light Years and is also nominated for Highest Selling Album and Album Of The Year, as well as Single Of The Year for 'On A Night Like This'.

Nov 6: Kylie appears at the MTV Europe Music Awards held at the Festhalle, Frankfurt, Germany

2002

Feb 20: Kylie wins two awards at the BRIT Awards; Best International Female Artist and Best International Album, for *Fever*.

Mar 6: At the 14th Annual World Music Awards, Kylie wins an award as Best Selling Australian Artist.

Apr 26: Start of the Kylie Fever 2002 Tour, with a concert in Cardiff, Wales. The tour went on

to cover England, Scotland, Sweden, Norway, Denmark, Germany, Austria, Switzerland, The Netherlands, France and Italy before moving to Australia.

Jul 23: The third waxwork version of Kylie is unveiled at Madame Tussauds. It shows her kneeling on all fours dressed in a skimpy red costume. The following month, after a complaint from Kylie who felt the pose was rather too revealing, the back of the dress was lengthened.

Aug 16: Last concert on the Kylie Fever 2002 Tour, in Melbourne, Australia.

Aug 29: Kylie wins an MTV Award in New York for best choreography for 'Can't Get You Out Of My Head'.

Oct 15: At the 16th Annual ARIA Awards, Kylie wins the Outstanding Achievement Award as well as Best Pop Release and Highest Selling Album for *Fever*, and Highest Selling Single and Single of The Year for 'Can't Get You Out Of My Head'. She is also nominated for Album Of The Year and Best Female Artist for *Fever*.

Oct 31: Kylie appears on BBC television's *Top Of The Pops* to perform her new single.

Nov: William Baker, Kylie's creative director, and Kylie release their book, *Kylie La La La*.

Nov 14: At the 2002 MTV Europe Music Awards held in Barcelona, Spain, Kylie wins Best Pop Act and Best Dance Act.

Nov 29: At the Top of the Pops awards held in Manchester, England, Kylie wins the award for Top Tour.

Dec 2: Kylie performs in The Royal Variety Performance at the Apollo Theatre in London, held in aid of the Entertainment Artistes Benevolent Fund.

Dec 12: The annual 2100 Jingle Ball concert at Madison Square Garden in New York features a performance by Kylie.

Dec 19: Kylie also appears at the KIIS FM Jingle Ball concert in Anaheim, California.

2003

Feb 4: UK launch of a new range of lingerie, LoveKylie.

Feb 20: Justin Timberlake and Kylie perform a raunchy routine at the 2003 BRIT Awards at Earls Court 2 in London.

Feb: Kylie finally ends her on-off relationship with James Gooding, who proceeds to sell his story to the UK tabloids.

Feb 23: Kylie meets French actor Olivier Martinez after the Grammy Awards in New York; he will become her new boyfriend.

Mar 9: The UK newspaper *News Of The World* publishes James Gooding's 'kiss and tell' story about his relationship with Kylie.

Apr: Kids Help Line, Optus and Kylie win an award for excellence from the Fundraising Institute of Australia for the 2002 fundraising campaign in Australia.

May 20: Olivier Martinez and Kylie appear officially for the first time as a couple at the Laureus World Sports Awards in Monaco.

Oct 17: The debut performance of Kylie's new single, 'Slow' on *Top Of The Pops*, which reveals a new image.

Nov 17: Kylie releases her 9th studio album *Body Language*.

2004

Jan: A Kylie Minogue poseable doll, available in two different outfits, is launched at the 51st Annual Toy Fair in London.

Feb 8: Kylie wins Best Dance Recording for 'Come Into My World' at the 48th Annual Grammy Awards in Los Angeles.

Oct: Tickets go on sale for the forthcoming Showgirl: The Greatest Hits Tour and sell out in two hours.

Dec: A celebrity nativity scene at Madame Tussauds features Kylie as the angel hovering over the stable. It also shows David and Victoria Beckham as Joseph and Mary; British Prime Minister Tony Blair, The Duke of Edinburgh and US President George W. Bush as the Three Wise Men; and Samuel L. Jackson, Hugh Grant and Graham Norton as the Shepherds.

2005

Jan 30: London première of *The Magic Roundabout* at Leicester Square. Kylie is the voice of Florence.

Feb 15: Kylie receives a Lifetime Achievement Award at the *Elle* Style Awards 2005

Mar 19: Start of the Showgirl: The Greatest Hits Tour with a concert in Glasgow, Scotland. It goes on to cover France, The Netherlands, Belgium, Austria, Germany, Switzerland, Denmark, Germany, Ireland and England. Further concerts were booked in Australia, Singapore and Hong Kong.

May 7: A film of Kylie's first Showgirl concert at Earls Court is broadcast on UK television's Channel 4, including a short backstage documentary section called *Behind The Feathers*. The film is later released as a DVD, *Showgirl – The Greatest Hits Tour*.

May 7: Final UK show in the Showgirl: The Greatest Hits Tour, in London, England.

May 17: It is announced that Kylie has early stage breast cancer; she cancels the remaining dates on her Showgirl: The Greatest Hits Tour and prepares to undergo surgery immediately.

Jul: Kylie begins chemotherapy in Paris, where she will be close to Olivier Martinez.

Dec 18: Final session of chemotherapy in Paris.

2006

Jan: Back in Australia, Kylie begins 6 months of radiation treatment that aims to prevent the cancer from returning.

Mar: Kylie visits Sri Lanka in the aftermath of the tsunami.

Jul: Olivier and Kylie visit Portofino in Italy for a short holiday.

Aug: Rehearsals start for the soon-to-be-resumed Showgirl tour.

Sep 16: Kylie appears to introduce the Scissor Sisters at their free gig in Trafalgar Square, London.

Sep 21: Publication of *The Showgirl Princess*, a children's book by Kylie.

Nov 8: Australian launch of Kylie's new fragrance Darling by Coty, in Sydney.

Nov 11: Start of the Showgirl: The Homecoming Tour with a concert in Sydney, Australia. The tour was a resumption of the Showgirl: The Greatest Hits Tour, which had been cancelled in 2005, and covered the major cities in Australia before moving to England for the New Year.

Dec 31: First UK concert of the Showgirl: The Homecoming Tour, at Wembley Arena in London.

2007

Jan 9: Kylie unveils a bronze cast of her hands at Wembley Arena's Square of Fame, where artists including Madonna and Sir Cliff Richard are also honoured.

Jan 10: The fourth version of Kylie is put on show at Madame Tussauds in London, the first scented waxwork since it is perfumed with the star's new scent, Darling. The model wears a long red dress and is shown sitting on a sparkling crescent moon, based on a scene from Showgirl: The Homecoming Tour. It made

Kylie the most-modelled person at Madame Tussauds except for the Queen.

Jan 23: Final concert in the Showgirl: The Homecoming Tour, held at the Manchester Evening News Arena in Manchester.

Feb 3: The relationship between Olivier Martinez and Kylie comes to an end, although they remain friends.

Feb 6: Kylie – The Exhibition opens at the V&A in London showcasing costumes from throughout her career.

Jul 7: Kylie performs in the Gay Parade concert at the Plaza de Espana, Madrid.

Aug: Launch of a second Kylie perfume, a softer version of the first called Sweet Darling

Oct 29: Kylie becomes the first recipient of the award for most radio plays of a female artist on British radio over the last 20 years, at the 2007 Music Industry Trust Awards

Nov 27: The UK's BBC Radio 2 broadcasts *X-amining Kylie: David Tennant in Conversation With Kylie Minogue*.

Dec 25: UK broadcast of the famous UK series Dr Who Christmas Special, 'Voyage Of The Damned', co-starring Kylie with David Tennant as the Doctor.

Dec 29: It is announced in the Queen's New Year's Honours List that Kylie will be awarded an OBE for services to music.

2008

Jan 28: Mika presents Kylie with a Lifetime Achievement Award at the NRJ Music Awards in Cannes.

Feb 5: UK launch of a range of bedlinen, Kylie At Home, in London.

Feb 9: David Tennant presents Kylie with the International Female Solo Artist Award at the 2008 BRIT Awards, held a in London.

May 5: French Culture Minister awards Kylie with the Chevalier of the Order of Arts and Letters at a ceremony in Paris.

May 6: Start of the KylieX2008 Tour with a concert in Paris. The tour covered most of Europe throughout June and July.

Jul 3: Kylie attends Buckingham Palace to receive her OBE from the Prince of Wales.

Aug 4: The last show on the first leg of the KylieX2008 Tour is held at the 02 Arena in London.

Oct: Kylie meets Andrés Velencoso.

Nov 1: The KylieX2008 Tour begins again in South America, with a concert in Bogotá, Colombia. Over the rest of the year it moves across South America and Asia, then moves on to Australasia.

Dec 8: Start of the KylieX2008 Tour in Australasia with a concert in Aukland, New Zealand.

Dec 11: Australian launch of a third Kylie fragrance, Sexy Darling, at Myer City Store, Sydney.

Dec 22: Final concert in the second leg of the KylieX2008 Tour is held at the Rod Laver Arena in Kylie's hometown of Melbourne, Victoria.

2009

Mar 14: Kylie appears at the Melbourne Sound Relief bushfire benefit – and was beamed live to the one in Sydney – to sing 'I Still Call Australia Home'.

Mar: Kylie launches a fourth new perfume, Couture, in association with Coty Beauty.

Apr: During a short holiday in Australia, Kylie takes new boyfriend Andrés Velencoso to meet her family.

May 2: The KylieX2008 Tour begins again in Europe, with material being performed at a concert in Ischgl, Austria. This leg goes on to cover Morocco, Poland, Spain, Portugal and Denmark.

May: Kylie launches a new fragrance for men, Inverse, with adverts starring her new man, Andrés Velencoso.

Jun 2: Racing driver Jensen Button presents Kylie with the Woman of the Year Award at the Glamour Women of the Year Awards 2009 in London.

Jul 27: Kylie appears on *The Today Show* in the US to promote her forthcoming tour of North America.

Aug 6: Final concert in the third leg of the KylieX2008 Tour is held in Skanderborg, Denmark.

Sep 7: UK launch of a new range of bed linen, Kylie At Home.

Sep 13: Kylie performs at Thank You For The Music, a celebration of the music of Abba in Hyde Park, London.

Sep 30: Start of the For You, For Me Tour, Kylie's first across North America, with a concert in Oakland. It also covered Las Vegas, Los Angeles, Chicago and Toronto, finishing with three concerts in New York City.

Oct 13: Last concert on the For You, For Me Tour, at the Hammerstein Ballroom in New York City.

Nov 28: In a list of the 25 Most Influential Australians put together by *Good Weekend*, Kylie made No.20.

2010

Feb 7: First date for digital download of 'Everybody Hurts', a charity single made to raise funds for earthquake victims in Haiti, featuring Kylie Minogue, Rod Stewart, Robbie Williams and Susan Boyle, amongst others.

Jun 3: The inaugural amfAR Inspiration Gala is hosted by Kylie at the New York Public Library and honours Jean-Paul Gaultier for his lifelong contribution to men's fashion and the fight against AIDS.

Jun 25: On BBC1's *Tonight With Jonathan Ross*, Kylie announces that she will tour again in 2011.

Jun 26: Kylie appears at the 40th Glastonbury Festival, performing with Jake Shears and Ana Matronic of the Scissor Sisters on the Pyramid Stage.

Jul 1: Pink Sparkle, Kylie's new perfume, goes on sale for the first time.

Jul 2: Release of *Aphrodite* in Australia and some European countries; it is released in the UK and other countries on July 5 and in the USA the following day.

Jul 21: An appearance on *Hey Hey, It's Saturday* is Kylie's first performance on Australian television for 10 years.

Nov 21: A flash mob forms to perform Kylie and Dannii's hits on the steps of Sydney Opera House.

Nov 25: Kylie appears in the famous Macy's Thanksgiving Parade in New York City.

2011

Feb 19: Start of the Aphrodite: Les Folies Tour in Herning, Denmark. The tour is scheduled to cover most of Europe and then move on to North America.

Apr 12: The European leg of the Aphrodite: Les Folies Tour finishes with a concert at the O2 Arena in London.

Apr 28: After 3 concerts in Japan, The Aphrodite: Les Folies Tour begins again in North America, with a concert in Montreal, Canada. In June and July it goes on the Australia and Asia.

July 14: The Aphrodite Tour comes to a close with a concert in Cape Town, South Africa.

Sep: Kylie begins filming *Holy Motors*, a film by French director Leos Carax.

2012

Mar 18: The Anti-Tour kicks off with a concert in Melbourne, Australia.

Jun 4: Kylie appears at Queen Elizabeth II's Diamond Jubilee Concert in London.

DISCOGRAPHY

1988

Kylie – release date: July 4, highest chart position: 1

1989

Enjoy Yourself – release date: October 9, highest chart position: 1

Kylie's Remixes Vol. 1 – compilation, release date: 13th February 13

1990

Rhythm Of Love – release date: November 11, highest chart position: 9

1991

Let's Get To It – release date: October 14, highest chart position: 15

1992

Kylie: Greatest Hits – compilation, release date: August 22

1994

Kylie Minogue – release date: September 19, highest chart position: 4

Non Stop History 50+1 – compilation, release date: April 4

1997

Greatest Remix Hits 1 – compilation, release date: January 20

Greatest Remix Hits 2 – compilation, release date: January 20

1998

Impossible Princess – release date: Mar 23, highest chart position: 10

Impossible Remixes – compilation, release date: July 8 (Australia only)

Mixes – compilation, release date: August 3

Greatest Remix Hits 3 – compilation, release date: August 21

Greatest Remix Hits 4 – compilation, release date: August 21

2000

Light Years – release date: September 25, highest chart position: 2

2001

Fever – release date: October 1, highest chart position: 1

2002

Kylie's Remixes Vol. 2 – compilation, release date: March 9

2003

Body Language – release date: November 17

2004

Ultimate Kylie – compilation, release date: November 22

2005

Showgirl – release date: November 28, highest chart position: 2

2007

X – release date: November 26, highest chart position: 4

2008

Kylie Boombox – compilation, release date: December 17

2009

Kylie Live in New York – digital download, release date: Dec 14

2010

Aphrodite – release date: July 2 (Australia), July 5 (UK), July 6 (US)

SINGLES

1987

'Locomotion' (Original) – release date: July 28

'I Should Be So Lucky' – release date: December 29

1988

'Got To Be Certain' – release date: July 2

'The Loco-Motion' (revised) – release date: July 25

'Je Ne Sais Pas Pourquoi' – release date: October 17

'Especially For You' – release date: November 28

'It's No Secret' – release date: December 15 (Japan & North America only)

'Turn It Into Love' – release date: December 21 (Japan only)

1989

'Hand On Your Heart' – release date: April 24

'Wouldn't Change A Thing' – release date: July 24

'Never Too Late' – release date: October 23

1990

 'Tears On My Pillow' – release date: January 8

'Better The Devil You Know' – release date: April 30

'Step Back In Time' – release date: October 22

1991

'What Do I Have To Do' – release date: January 21

'Shocked' – release date: May 20

'Word Is Out' – release date: August 26

'If You Were With Me Now' – release date: October 14

'Keep On Pumpin' It' – release date: November 4

1993

 'Give Me Just A Little More Time' – release date: January 13

'Finer Feelings' – release date: April 13

 'What Kind Of Fool' – release date: August 10

 'Celebration' – release date: November 16

1994

'Confide In Me' – release date: September 5

 'Put Yourself In My Place' – release date: November 21

1995

'Where Is The Feeling' – release date: July 17

'Where The Wild Roses Grow' (with Nick Cave) – release date: October 9

1997

'Some Kind of Bliss' – release date: September 15

'Did It Again' – release date: December 1

'GBI' (with Towa Tei) – release date: Japan only December, worldwide October 26

1998

'Breathe' – release date: March 16

'Cowboy Style' – release date: August (Australia only)

2000

 'Spinning Around' – release date: June 19

'On A Night Like This' – release date: September 11

'Kids' (with Robbie Williams) – release date: October 9

'Please Stay' – release date: December 11

2001

 'Your Disco Needs You' – release date: Germany and limited edition Australia only February 19

'Can't Get You Out Of My Head' – release date: September 17

'Butterfly' – release date: US only November 12

2002

'In Your Eyes' – release date: February 18

'Love At First Sight' – release date: June 10

'Come Into My World' – release date: November 2 Australia, November 11 UK

2003

'Slow' – release date: November 3

2004

'Red Blooded Woman' – release date: March 5

'Chocolate' – release date: June 28

'I Believe In You' – release date: December 6

2005

'Giving You Up' – release date: March 28

2007

'2 Hearts' – release date: November 12

2008

'Wow' – release date: February 18

'All I See' – release date: May 5

'In My Arms' – release date: May 5

'The One' – release date: digital single only July 28

2010

'All The Lovers' – release date: digital download June 13, general release July 5

'Get Outta My Way' – release date: September 27

'Better Than Today' – release date: digital download December 5

2011

'Put Your Hands Up (If You Feel Love)' – release date May 29

2012

'Timebomb' – release date May 25

VIDEO & DVD

1989

Kylie: The Videos I – release date: November

Kylie: The Videos II – release date: November

1990

Kylie On The Go: Live In Japan – release date: April

1991

Let's Get To...The Videos – release date: December

1992

Kylie: Live In Dublin – release date: April

Kylie Minogue: Greatest Hits – release date: August

1998

The Kylie Tapes 94–98 – release date: August

2000

Kylie Minogue: Live In Sydney – release date: October

2002

Fever: Live In Manchester – release date: November 18

2004

Body Language Live – release date: July 12

Ultimate Kylie – release date: November 22

2005

Showgirl: Greatest Hits Tour – release date: November 28

2007

White Diamond – release date: December 10

TELEVISION & FILMS

1980

Skyways Episode 58

The Sullivans Episodes 637–644

1985

The Zoo Family Episode 23

The Henderson Kids Episodes 1–24

1986

Fame and Misfortune Episodes 1–6

1987

Neighbours Episodes 234–777

1989

The Delinquents – Australia release December 21, UK release December 26

1994

The Vicar Of Dibley Episode 3 – broadcast UK only November

Streetfighter: The Movie – First release December 23

1995

Hayride To Hell Arthouse film – no general release

1996

Bio-Dome – First release January 12

1997

Men Behaving Badly Comic Relief Special – broadcast UK only March

Misfit Arthouse film – broadcast UK only November

Diana & Me – released Australia only December

2000

Cut – First release March 2

Sample People – released Australia only May 11

2001

Moulin Rouge! – First release May 24

An Audience With Kylie Minogue – broadcast UK only October

2002

Kylie: La La La (or Feel The Fever) – broadcast UK only October

2004

Kath & Kim Season 3, Episodes 7–8 – broadcast Australia only November

2005

The Magic Roundabout (voice only) – First release February 2

2007

The Kylie Show – broadcast UK only November

Dr. Who 2007 Christmas Special 'Voyage of the Damned' – broadcast December

2009

Blue – First release October 16

2012

Jack and Diane – First released April 20

Holy Motors – First released July 4